Essential Ifa Reference

Baba Jaha Cummings

blue ocean press

tokyo

Published by: blue ocean press, an imprint of ARI

#807-36 Lions Plaza Ebisu

3-25-3 Higashi, Shibuya-ku

Tokyo, Japan 150-0011

Email: contact@blueoceanpublications.com

URL: http://www.blueoceanpublications.com

ISBN: 978-4-902837-04-9

Table of Contents

Introduction

This book was written to provide a reference to spiritual practioners and scholars who desire an essential overview of key elements in the practical application of Ifa.

Chapter 1 provides the names of the 256 Odus, the metaphysical principal they represent, the herbs associated with them, and the Orisha, Egun, or other Energies whom are speaking in the sign.

Chapter 2 provdes a description of the State of Consciousness that each of the Major Orisha embodies.

Chapter 3 provides an extensive list of herbs used in Ifa, in particular in the Americas. The list is arranged in alphabetical order of their scientific name. The Spanish name and the Yoruba of each are included as well.

Chapter 4 provldes a list of trees commonly used to make "palos" (sticks).

Chapter 1

List of 256 Odus

Each entry includes variations of the names of the odu. The odus are numbered in sequence, as to organize by books; but it should be noted that, in actuality, the 16 Mejis emerged first, followed by Oshe Otura, which brought into existence the other combinations.

1. Baba Ogbe, Baba Eyiogbe, Baba Eyiogbe Meyi

+

I I

I I

I I

I I

Principle: Creation of an open road, alignment with destiny, Iwa Pele

Herbs: Mangle Rojo, Palo Bobo, Itamo Real, Iroko, Orquidas, Ayua, Bejucubi, Guira, Ceiba, Cundiamor, Coralillo, Orozun

Orisha Speaking: Igba Iwa Odu, Oduduwa, Orishanla, Eshu, Yemaya, Olokun, Shango, Oshun

2. Ogbe Yekun, Ogbe Yeku

+

O I

O I

O I

O I

Principle: An open road leads to completion of a cycle

Herbs: Zapote Estefanote

Orisha Speaking: Oduduwa, Orunmila, Eshu, Oshun

3. Ogbe Iwori, Ogbe Wene

+

O I

I I

I I

O I

Principle: An open road leads to transformation

Herbs: Jobo, Sauco, Pierdo Rumbo

Orisha speaking: Eshu, Obatala, Shango, Olokun, Oshun, Egun, Oro, Aleyo

4. Ogbe Odi, Ogbe Di

+

I I

O I

O I

I I

Principle: An open road leads to rebirth

Herbs: Chirimoya, Guanina, Ceiba, Paraiso, Algodon, Moruro, Mangle Rojo, Lino

Orisha speaking: Eleggua, Obatala, Ogun, Oshun, Dada, Orunmila, Eleda, Oke

5. Ogbe Irosun, Ogbe Roso, Oberoso

+

I I

I I

O I

O I

Principle: An open road leads to fulfillment of creative potential

Herbs: Cucaracha, Cordovan, Pino Africano, Don Chayo, Ojo de Buey

Orisha speaking: Orunmila, Eshu, Ogun, Osanyin, Olokun, Egungun

6. Ogbe Owonrin, Ogbe Ojuani, Ogbe Juani, Ogbe Wale

+

O I

O I

I I

I I

Principle: An open road creates an unexpected outcome

Herbs: Malanga, Chamico, Carolina, Tua tua, Hierba Buena, Guama, Zarzaparilla

Orisha speaking: Orunmila, Eshu, Egun, Obatala

7. Ogbe Obara, Ogbe Bara

+

I I

O I

O I

O I

Principle: An open road leads to self-transformation

Herbs: Hiedara, Frijol Caballero, Avallano, Fruita de Pan

Orisha speaking: Shango, Orunmila, Obatala

8. Ogbe Okanran, Ogbe Okana, Ogbe Kana

+

O I

O I

O I

I I

Principle: An open road creates a new direction

Herbs: Needle Cactus, Cardon, Añil

Orisha speaking: Agboniregun, Eshu, Orungan, Orishabi, Obatala, Shango, Egun, Eleda

9. Ogbe Ogunda, Ogbe Yono

+

I I

I I

I I

O I

Principle: An open road leads to conflict (or removal of obstacles)

Herbs: Jobo, Eleboyuye, Atiponia, Siguaraya, Moruro, Piño, and Prodijosa

Orisha speaking: Orunmila, Eshu, Ekunlempe, Kebioso, Obatala, Ogun, Aje

10. Ogbe Osa, Ogbe Sa

+

O I

I I

I I

I I

Principle: An open road creates sudden change

Herbs: Jaboncillo, Ceiba. Sauco Blanco, Pasiflor, Moruro

Orisha speaking: Shango, Obatala, Oduduwa, Oshun, Eshu, Yemaya, Olokun, Olofin

11. Ogbe Ika, Ogbe Ka

<pre>
          +
         O I
         I I
         O I
         O I
</pre>

Principle: An open road leads to a gathering of Asé

Herbs: Garro, Salvadera, Iwereyeye

Orisha speaking: Orunmila, Eshu, Ogun

12. Ogbe Otrupon, Ogbe Trupon

<pre>
          +
         O I
         O I
         I I
         O I
</pre>

Principle: An open road leads to good health (or disease)

Herbs: Bleo Blanco, Frescura, Verdolaga, Peregun, Atiponla

Orisha speaking: Orunmila, Eshu, Shango, Babaluaye

13. Ogbe Otura, Ogbe Tura

+

I I

O I

I I

I I

Principle: An open road creates spiritual consciousness

Herbs: Cucaracha, Quita Maledicion, Albahaca, Orosun

Orisha speaking: Eshu, Orunmila, Oduduwa, Igba Iwa Odu, Obatala, Iroko, Ogun

14. Ogbe Irete, Ogbe Ate

+

I I

I I

O I

I I

Principle: An open road creates determination

Herbs: Cardon, Gandul, Canistel, Verbena, Boton de Oro

Orisha speaking: Oduduwa, Igba Iwa Odu, Obatala, Oshun, Shango, Eshu, Osanyin, Ogun

15. Ogbe Oshe, Ogbe She

+

I I

O I

I I

O I

Principle: An open road leads to fertility

Herbs: Artemisa, Piño

Orisha speaking: Eshu, Obatala, Oshun, Orunmila, Ti-Ile, Osanyin, Ogun

16. Ogbe Ofun, Ogbe Fun

+

O I

I I

O I

I I

Principle: An open road leads to a miracle

Herbs: Algodo, Prodijiosa, Moruro, Pomarrosa

Orisha speaking: Obatala, Olodumare, Eshu, Iku, Orunmila, Ogun, Oshun

17. Baba Oyeku Meyi, Baba Oyekun Meji

+

O O

O O

O O

O O

Principle: The end of cycles, end of a cycle

Herbs: Marpacifico, Osun, Ewe aro, Algarrobo, Pendejera

Orisha speaking: Shango, Orunmila, Iku, Eshu, Ibejis, Babaluaye, Olofin

18. Oyeku Ogbe, Oyekun Ogbe

+

I O

I O

I O

I O

Principle: End of a cycle creates an open road

Herbs: Higo

Orisha speaking: Olofin, Eshu, Oranfe, Shango, Obatala, Olokun, Ibejis

19. Oyeku Iwori, Oyekun Iwori, Oyekun Wori

+

O O

I O

I O

O O

Principle: End of a cycle leads to transformation

Herbs: Boton de oro, Lino de Rio, Miliflores, Hiedra, Ewe Ayo

Orisha speaking: Orunmila, Shango, Oshun, Abiku, Olofin, Ibejis

20. Oyeku Odi, Oyekun Odi, Oyekun Di

+

I O

O O

O O

I O

Principle: End of a cycle creates rebirth

Herbs: Mandarina, Lima, Naranja

Orisha speaking: Orunmila

21. Oyeku Irosu, Oyekun Irosun, Oyekun Biroso

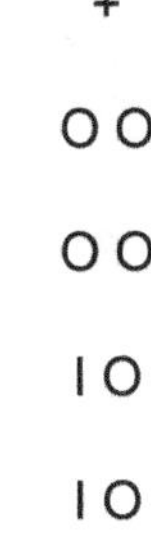

Principle: End of a cycle leads to fulfillment of creative potential

Herbs: Panetela, Odan

Orisha speaking: Orunmila, Olofin, Awos, Shango

22. Oyeku Owonrin, Oyekun Ojuani, Oyekun Juani

Principle: End of a cycle creates unexpected change

Herbs: Melon de Castilla, Jaguey

Orisha speaking: Eshu, Sakpata (Sakpate), Shango, Ogun

23. Oyekun Obara, Oyekun Bara

+

I O

O O

O O

O O

Principle: End of a cycle leads to self-transformation

Herbs: Jonjoto, Bejuco Garanon, Bejuco Congo

Orisha speaking: Eshu, Obatala, Olofin, Shango, Ogun, Yemaya

24. Oyeku Okanran, Oyekun Okana, Oyekun Kana

+

O O

O O

O O

I O

Principle: End of a cycle creates a new direction

Herbs: Jara Jara, Itamo Real, Yagruma, Paraiso, Prodijiosa

Orisha speaking: Eshu, Egun, Shango, Oduduwa, Aiye Shaluga

25. Oyekun Ogunda, Oyekun Gunda

+

I O

I O

I O

O O

Principle: End of a cycle leads to conflict (or removal of obstacles)

Herbs: Bejuco Berraco, Hierba de niña, Ewe Oguma

Orisha speaking: Orunmila, Ogun, Obatala, Oya

26. Oyeku Osa, Oyekun Osa, Oyekun Sa

+

O O

I O

I O

I O

Principle: End of a cycle creates sudden change

Herbs: Alamo, Ewe Odan

Orisha speaking: Orunmila, Oya, Ogun, Oshosi

27. Oyeku Ika, Oyekun Ika, Oyekun Ka

```
           +
          O O
          I O
          O O
          O O
```

Principle: End of a cycle creates a gathering of Asé

Herbs: Romerillo, Paraguita, Palo Brasillete

Orisha speaking: Orunmila, Eshu, Shango, Ogun, Obatala, Ibejis

28. Oyeku Oturupon, Oyekun Otrupon, Oyekun Trupo

```
           +
          O O
          O O
          I O
          O O
```

Principle: End of cycles leads to good health (or disease)

Herbs: Cerezo, Melon

Orisha speaking: Orunmila, Ogun, Eshu, Yalorde

29. Oyeku Otura, Oyekun Otura, Oyekun Tesia

+

IO

OO

IO

IO

Principle: End of a cycle creates spiritual consciousness

Herbs: Cambia Voz, Palo Guachinango

Orisha speaking: Olorun, Olokun, Orunmila, Aroni, Ogun, Shango, Elegba

30. Oyeku Irete, Oyekun Irete, Oyekun Birete

+

I O

I O

O O

I O

Principle: End of a cycle creates determination

Herbs: Tomate de Guinea, Berro, Ewe Oguma

Orisha speaking: Babaluaye, Oshun, Eshu, Ogun, Egun, Shango

31. Oyeku Ose, Oyekun Oshe, Oyekun Pakioshe

+

I O

O O

I O

O O

Principle: End of a cycle creates fertility

Herbs: Malva de Cochino, Malvate

Orisha speaking: Iku, Eshu, Olofin, Shango, Egun

32. Oyeku Ofun

+

O O

I O

O O

I O

Principle: End of a cycle creates a miracle

Herbs: Ojo de Raton, Albahaca morada, Yerba Fina

Orisha speaking: Shango, Eshu, Oya

33. Baba Iwori Meji, Baba Iwori Meyi

<pre>
        +
       O O
       I I
       I I
       O O
</pre>

Principle: Transformation, passion, fire

Herbs: Pitahaya, Bleo Blanco, Cardo Santo

Orisha speaking: Orunmila, Eshu, Olofin, Oshun, Osanyin, Olokun

34. Iwori Ogbe, Iwori Bogbe

<pre>
        +
       I O
       I I
       I I
       I O
</pre>

Principle: Transformation creates an open road

Herbs: Zazafra, Pata de gallina, Ceiba, Almasigo, Tuna

Orisha speaking: Orunmila, Oshun, Olokun, Shnago, Eshu, Ibejis

35. Iwori Oyeku, Iwori Oyekun, Iwori Yeku

+

O O

O I

O I

O O

Principle: Transformation leads to end of a cycle

Herbs: Momoncillo, Jocuma

Orisha speaking: Egungun, Eshu, Oshun, Yemaya, Orunmila, Irunmoles

36. Iwori Odi, Iwori Di, Iwori Bodi

+

I O

O I

O I

I O

Principle: Transformation leads to rebirth

Herbs: Jiba, Malambo, Flor de Aqua, Cocuyo

Orisha speaking: Obatala, Ogun, Orunmila

37. Iwori Irosun, Iwori Irosu, Iwori Koso

+

I O

I I

O I

O O

Principle: Transformation leads to fulfillment of creative potential

Herbs: Palma, Iroko, Majagua

Orisha speaking: Orunmila, Osun, Eshu, Oduduwa, Olokun, Orisha Oko, Yewa, Agayu

38. Iwori Owonrin, Iwori Ojuani

+

O O

O I

I I

I O

Principle: Transformation creates an unexpected outcome

Herbs: Atiponla, Tusa de Maiz

Orisha speaking: Osanyin, Obatala, Shango, Orunmila, Yemaya

39. Iwori Obara, Iwori Bere

+

I O

O I

O I

O O

Principle: Transformation leads to self-transformation

Herbs: Pica Pica, Algodon

Orisha speaking: Orunmila, Olofin, Osun, Osanyin, Eshu, Oshun, Shango, Eshu

40. Iwori Okanran, Iwori Okana, Iwori Kana

+

O O

O I

O I

I O

Principle: Transformation creates a new direction

Herbs: Ashibata, Guama, Iworiyeye

Orisha speaking: Orunmila, Olokun, Obatala, Ogun, Yemaya

41. Iwori Ogunda, Iwori Gunda

+

I O

I I

I I

O O

Principle: Transformation leads to conflict (or removal of obstacles)

Herbs: Guisaso de Caballo, Higuereta

Orisha speaking: Obatala, Shango, Ogun, Orunmila, Yemaya, Eshu, Orun

42. Iwori Osa, Iwori Bosa

+

O O

I I

I I

I O

Principle: Transformation creates sudden change

Herbs: Salvia, Piñon de Botija

Orisha speaking: Orunmila, Eshu, Obatala, Shango, Oya, Ogun, Oshosi, Oshun, Iku

43. Iwori Ika, Iwori Boka

```
        +
       O O
       | |
       O |
       O O
```

Principle: Transformation leads to gathering of Asé

Herbs: Jagua, Paraiso, Alamo

Orisha speaking: Orunmila, Oshun, Orishanla, Olofin

44. Iwori Oturupon, Iwori Otrupon, Iwori Batuto

```
        +
       O O
       O |
       | |
       O O
```

Principle: Transformation leads to good health (or disease)

Herbs: Tua Tua, Algarrobo, Ewe Ayo

Orisha speaking: Orunmila, Olokun, Yemaya, Shango, Ala

45. Iwori Otura, Iwori Turale

<pre>
      +
    I O
    O I
    I I
    I O
</pre>

Principle: Transformation leads to spiritual consciousness

Herbs: Mejorana, Levantate

Orisha speaking: Shango, Eshu, Orunmila

46. Iwori Irete, Iwori Rote

<pre>
      +
    I O
    I I
    O I
    I O
</pre>

Principle: Transformation creates determination

Herbs: Vinagrillo

Orisha speaking: Orunmila, Oshun, Shango, Obatala

47. Iwori Ose, Iwori Oshe, Iwori Boshe

+

I O

O I

I I

O O

Principle: Transformation creates fertility

Herbs: Incienza de Guinea

Orisha speaking: Orunmila, Olorun, Oshun, Yemaya, Olokun, Obatala

48. Iwori Ofun, Iwori Bofun

+

O O

I I

O I

I O

Principle: Transformation creates a miracle

Herbs: Palo Tocino, Uña de Gato, Acacia

Orisha speaking: Olofin, Egungun, Orunmila, Eshu, Yemaya, Ogun, Shango

49. Baba Odi Meji, Baba Odi Meyi

+

I I

O O

O O

I I

Principle: Creates rebirth

Herbs: Flor de Aroma, Amansaguapo, Alamo, Atiponla, Jaguey, Higo, Laurel

Orisha speaking: Orunmila, Yemaya, Obatala, Eshu, Osanyin, Ogun, Oshun, Egungun

50. Odi Ogbe, Edigbe, Edible, Edibere

+

I I

I O

I O

I I

Principle: Rebirth creates an open road

Herbs: Jaguey, Cerezo, Ruda, Tapacamino

Orisha speaking: Shango, Oduduwa, Obatala, Orunmila, Eshu, Oya, Ogun, 7 African Powers

51. Odi Oyeku, Odi Oyekun, Odi Yeku

+

O I

O O

O O

O I

Principle: Rebirth leads to end of a cycle

Herb: Caña de Castillo, Dagame, Ateje

Orisha speaking: Orunmila, Oya, Shango, Obatala, Olokun

52. Odi Iwori, Odi Wori, Odi Oro

+

O I

I O

I O

O I

Principle: Rebirth creates transformation

Herbs: Oju Oro, Flor de Agua

Orisha speaking: Ela (Agboniregun), Obalufe, Shango, Oro, Oshun, Yemaya, Obatala

53. Odi Irosun, Odi Iroso

+

I I

I O

O O

O I

Principle: Rebirth leads to fulfillment of creative potential

Herbs: Esparto, Atiponla, Guira Cimarrona, Majagua

Orisha speaking: Orunmila, Orishanla, Ogun, Oshun, Olofin, Egungun

54. Odi Owonrin, Odi Ojuani, Odi Juani, Odi Moni

+

O I

O O

I O

I I

Principle: Rebirth creates an unexpected outcome

Herbs: Ñame

Orisha speaking: Orunmila, Olofin, Obatala, Apetebi, Shango

55. Odi Obara, Odi Bara

\+

I I

O O

O O

O I

Principle: Rebirth leads to self-transformation

Herbs: Peonia, Mani, Verdolaga, Platanillo de Cuba

Orisha speaking: Orunmila, Shango, Yemaya, Obatala, Ogun

56. Odi Okanran, Odi Okana, Odi Kana

\+

O I

O O

O O

O I

Principle: Rebirth creates a new direction

Herbs: Corojo, Caimito, Caña Brava, Yierba Raton

Orisha speaking: Orunmila, Eshu, Olokun, Olodumare, Shango, Oshun, Afe, Orisha-Oko

57. Odi Ogunda, Odi Gunda

+

I I

I O

I O

O I

Principle: Rebirth leads to conflict (or removal of obstacles)

Herbs: Pitahaya, Alamo, Orozun, Romesaraguey, Paraiso, Quita Maldicion, Algodon, Jobo

Orisha speaking: Orunmila, Ogun, Yemaya, Oshun, Eshu

58. Odi Osa, Odi Sa

+

O I

I O

I O

I I

Principle: Rebirth creates sudden change

Herbs: Boton de Oro, Orozun, Romerillo, Prodijiosa

Orisha speaking: Yemaya, Orunmila, Eshu, Olofin, Egun, Ogun

59. Odi Ika, Odi Ka

+

O I

I O

O O

O I

Principle: Rebirth leads to a gathering of Asé

Herbs: Yaguma, Alamo, Paraiso, Calabaza, Ewe Buye

Orisha speaking: Orunmila, Ori, Oduduwa, Oro, Eshu, Olokun, Igbe Iwa Odu

60. Odi Oturupon, Odi Otrupon, Odi Trupon, Odi Batrupon

+

O I

O O

I O

O I

Principle: Rebirth creates good health (or disease)

Herbs: Parra Cimarrona, Cundiamor, Platano, Colonia

Orisha speaking: Olofin, Orunmila, Shango, Yemaya, Oshun, Eshu

61. Odi Otura, Odi Tura, Odi Tauro

+
I I
O O
I O
I I

Principle: Rebirth creates spiritual consciousness

Herbs: Alamo, Seso Vegetal, Datil

Orisha speaking: Obatala, Eshu, Orunmila, Egun, Shango, Inle, Oshun

62. Odi Irete, Odi Rete, Odi Leke

+
I I
I O
O O
I I

Principle: Rebirth leads to determination

Herbs: Guasima, Guayabita

Orisha speaking: Orunmila, Oshun, Olokun, Yemaya, Eshu, Ibejis

63. Odi Ose, Odi Oshe, Odi She

+

I I

O O

I O

O I

Principle: Rebirth leads to fertility

Herbs: Zazafran

Orisha speaking: Orunmila, Oshosi, Oshun, Olofin, Eshu

64. Odi Ofun, Odi Fun, Odi Fumbo

+

O I

I O

O O

I I

Principle: Rebirth creates a miracle

Herbs: Algodon, Guaracabuya

Orisha speaking: Orunmila, Eshu, Obatala, Egun, Babaluaye

65. Baba Irosun Meji, Baba Iroso Meyi

+

I I

I I

O O

O O

Principle: Fulfillment of creative potential

Herbs: Ewe Ayo, Acebo, Boton de Oro

Orisha speaking: Orunmila, Shango, Olokun, Yewa, Ibejis, Obatala, Yemaya

66. Irosun Ogbe, Iroso Ogbe, Iroso Umbo

+

I I

I I
I O

I O

Principle: Fulfillment of creative potential creates an open road

Herbs: Malva Blanca, Canutillo, Cucaracha, Almacigo, Algodon

Orisha speaking: Orunmila, Eshu, Yemaya, Olokun, Olofin, Ogun, Oshun

67. Irosun Oyeku, Irosu Oyekun, Irosu Yeku

+

O I

O I

O O

O O

Principle: Fulfillment of creative potential leads to end of a cycle

Herbs: Granda

Orisha speaking: Orunmila, Eshu, Osanyin, Shango

68. Irosun Iwori, Iroso Iwori

+

O I

I I

I O

O O

Principle: Fulfillment of creative potential leads to transformation

Herbs: Mamey, Palma, Jaguey, Quita Maldicion

Orisha speaking: Orunmila, Yewa, Shango, Agayu, Babaluaye

69. Irosun Odi, Irosu Odi, Irosu Di

+

I I

O I

O O

I O

Principle: Fulfillment of creative potential leads to rebirth

Herbs: Algodon, Ewe Fin, Platano Africano, Mala Cara, Cedro, Almendra

Orisha speaking: Orunmila, Obatala, Eshu, Shango, Oshun

70. Irosun Owonrin, Irosu Ojuani, Irosu Juani

+

O I

O I

I O

I O

Principle: Fulfillment of creative potential creates an unexpected outcome

Herbs: Adracana, Palma Real, Nitro Dulce, Pino

Orisha speaking: Eshu, Shango, Orunmila, Obatala, Oshun, Ogun, Oshosi, Osun

71. Irosun Obara, Iroso Obara, Iroso Bara, Iroso Gan

+

I I

O I

O O

O O

Principle: Fulfillment of creative potential leads to self-transformation

Herbs: Chamico, Bleo Blanco

Orisha speaking: Orunmila, Shango, Ibejis, Egungun, Oshun

72. Irosun Okanran, Iroso Okana, Iroso Kalu

+

O I

O I

O O

I O

Principle: Fulfillment of creative potential creates a new direction

Herbs: Estefaniote, Escamelote, Baston de San Francisco

Orisha speaking: Orunmila, Shango, Obatala Osun

73. Irosun Ogunda, Iroso Ogunda, Iroso Torda

\+

I I

I I

I O

O O

Principle: Fulfillment of creative potential leads to conflict (or removal of obstacles)

Herbs: Parra Cimarrona, Almendra, Hojas de Uva Caidas

Orisha speaking: Obatala, Ogun, Shango, Orunmila, Olokun

74. Irosun Osa, Iroso Osa, Iroso Bosa

\+

O I

I I

I O

I O

Principle: Fulfillment of creative potential creates sudden change

Herbs: Ceiba, Guayaba, Jaguey, Algarrobo, Alamo

Orisha speaking: Olofin, Irunmoles, Orunmila, Shango, Oshun, Obatala, Oya, Osun

75. Irosun Ika, Iroso Ika, Iroso Boka

+

O I

I I

O O

O O

Principle: Fulfillment of creative potential creates a gathering of Asé

Herbs: Atiponla, Malambo, Amansaguapo, Cabo de Hacha

Orisha speaking: Oshun, Eshu, Orunmila, Obatala, Ogun, Oshosi, Osun

76. Irosun Oturupon, Iroso Otrupon, Iroso Otrupo

+

O I

O I

I O

O O

Principle: Fulfillment of creative potential creates good health (or disease)

Herbs: Aji Guaguao, Pierde Rumbo, Yaya, Jiki, Jokuma, Moruro, Ayua, Laurel

Orisha speaking: Eshu, Elegba, Iroko, Oya, Oduduwa, Oro, Osanyin

77. Irosun Otura, Iroso Otura, Iroso Tura

+

I I

O I

I O

I O

Principle: Fulfillment of creative potential leads to spiritual consciousness

Herbs: Yaya, Algodon, Meloncillo

Orisha speaking: Eshu, Orunmila, Ogun, Oshun, Olofin, Obatala

78. Irosun Irete, Iroso Irete, Iroso Ate

+

I I

I I

O O

I O

Principle: Fulfillment of creative potential creates determination

Herbs: Salvia, Castaño, Caoba, Sabino, Amansaguapo, Cambia Voz

Orisha speaking: Orunmila, Olokun, Olofin, Obatala, Oshun

79. Irosun Ose, Iroso Oshe, Iroso Koshe

+

I I

O I

I O

O O

Principle: Fulfillment of creative potential creates fertility

Herbs: Esucho, Pandera, Tebeke, Ewe Efunle, Ahuinaldo Blanco

Orisha speaking: Eleda, Olodumare, Orunmila, Eshu, Iku, Shango, Agayu

80. Irosun Ofun, Iroso Ofun, Iroso Fun

+

O I

I I

O O

I O

Principle: Fulfillment of creative potential creates a miracle

Herbs: Ajonjoli, Frijoles Caballero, Hierba Seca

Orisha speaking: Orisha-nla, Orunmila, Oya, Eshu, Shango, Osun

81. Baba Owonrin Meji, Baba Ojuani Meyi

```
        +
       O O
       O O
       I I
       I I
```

Principle: Creates an unexpected outcome

Herbs: Jaboncillo, Majagua, Cundiamor

Orisha speaking: Eshu, Babaluaye, Orunmila, Osanyin, Aroni, Agangara, Nana Buruku, Oshosi, Iya

82. Owonrin Ogbe, Ojuani Ogbe, Ojuani Shogbe

```
        +
       I O
       I O
       I I
       I I
```

Principle: Unexpected outcome creates an open road

Herbs: Acelga, Col. Malanga, Algodon, Salvadera, Verdolaga Marino, Yamao, Yagruma

Orisha speaking: Eshu, Yalorde, Orunmila, Obatala, Oya, Babaluaye

83. Owonrin Oyeku, Ojuani Oyekun, Ojuani Yeku

+

O O

O O

O I

O I

Principle: Unexpected outcome leads to end of a cycle

Herbs: Framboyan, Roble, Caiman

Orisha speaking: Eshu, Oshun, Oya, Shango, Orunmila

84. Owonrin Iwori, Ojuani Iwori, Ojuani Tanshela

+

O O

I O

I I

O I

Principle: Unexpected outcome leads to transformation

Herbs: Corojo, Hedionda, Pata Gallina, Muralla, Yierba Cangrejo

Orisha speaking: Orunmila, Eshu, Oshun, Olorun, Babaluaye

85. Owonrin Odi, Ojuani Odi, Ojuani Shidi

+

I O

O O

O I

I I

Principle: Unexpected outcome leads to rebirth

Herbs: Valeriana, Yini, Ayeni, Esclariosa, Espinaca

Orisha speaking: Orunmila, Oshun, Odde, Babaluaye, Eshu, Osun

86. Owonrin Irosun, Ojuani Iroso, Ojuani Roso

+

I O

I O

O I

O I

Principle: Unexpected outcome leads to fulfillment of creative potential

Herbs: Ñame, Algodon, Moruro, Palo Cenizo, Diame, Daguilla

Orisha speaking: Obatala, Yewa, Shango, Orunmila, Eleggua

87. Owonrin Obara, Ojuani Obara, Ojuani Lozure

+

I O

O O

O I

O I

Principle: Unexpected outcome leads to self-transformation

Herbs: Peonia, Maravilla, Guira, Ewe Ogum

Orisha speaking: Orunmila, Obatala, Eshu, Ogun, Osanyin, Egun

88. Owonrin Okanran, Ojuani Okana, Ojuani Kana, Ojuani Pokon

+

O O

O O

O I

I I

Principle: Unexpected outcome creates a new direction

Herbs: Artemisa, Erete, Ristra de Ajo, Licopodio

Orisha speaking: Orunmila, Eshu, Oya, Oshun

89. Owonrin Ogunda, Ojuani Ogunda, Ojuani Gunda

+

I O

I O

I I

O I

Principle: Unexpected outcome leads to conflict (or removal of obstacles)

Herbs: Ceiba, Cipres, Guayaba Guinea, Palo Pimienta

Orisha speaking: Orunmila, Olofin, Oya, Obatala, Ogun, Obini

90. Owonrin Osa, Ojuani Osa, Ojuani Osa

+

O O

I O

I I

I I

Principle: Unexpected outcome creates sudden change

Herbs: Salvia, Malvate, Ciruela, Espartillo, Paraiso, Cedro Blanco, Vence Batalla

Orisha speaking: Orunmila, Eshu, Olofin, Obatala, Osanyin

91. Owonrin Ika, Ojuani Ika, Ojuani Ka

+

O O

I O

O I

O I

Principle: Unexpected outcome leads to a gathering of Asé

Herbs: Esponja, Aragba, Maiz, Granadillo, Jocuma, Quibra Hacha, Mirebolan

Orisha speaking: Eshu, Shango, Oshun, Olofin, Orunmila

92. Owonrin Oturupon, Ojuani Otrupon, Ojuani Trupo

+

O O

O O

I I

O I

Principle: Unexpected outcome creates good health (or disease)

Herbs: Palo Ashorin, Mano de Pilon, Copey

Orisha speaking : Eshu, Orunmila, Shango, Babaluaye

93. Owonrin Otura, Ojuani Otura, Ojuani Alakentu

+

I O

O O

I I

I I

Principle: Unexpected outcome leads to spiritual consciousness

Herbs: Caña Santo, Hierba Fina, Quimbansa, Hierba Raton

Orisha speaking: Eshu, Egungun, Yemaya, Orunmila, Olokun, Babaluaye, Oshosi, Oshun

94. Owonrin Irete, Ojuani Irete, Ojuani Birete

+

I O

I O

O I

I I

Principle: Unexpected outcome creates determination

Herbs: Alacrancillo, Berbana, Colonia, Higo, Algodon, Malvate

Orisha speaking: Eshu, Olokun, Olofin, Oshun, Orunmila

95. Owonrin Ose, Ojuani Oshe, Ojuani She, Ojuani Boshe

+

I O

O O

I I

O I

Principle: Unexpected outcome creates fertility

Herbs: Hierba Lechera, Estropajo, Hierba Nitro

Orisha speaking: Orunmila, Olokun, Obatala, Oshun

96. Owonrin Ofun, Ojuani Ofun, Ojuani Fun, Ojuani Bofun

+

O O

I O

O I

I I

Principle: Unexpected outcome creates a miracle

Herbs: Baga, Ñame

Orisha speaking: Orunmila, Eshu, Shango, Oshun, Obatala

97. Baba Obara Meji, Baba Obara Meyi

+

I I

O O

O O

O O

Principle: Creates self-transformation

Herbs: Lirio, Meloncillo

Orisha speaking: Orunmila, Shango, Elegba, Obatala, Olofin, Oshun

98. Obara Ogbe, Obara Bogbe

+

I I

I O

I O

I O

Principle: Self-transformation creates an open road

Herbs: Maloja, Piñon de Botjia, Picuala

Orisha speaking: Elegba, Osanyin, Orunmila, Obatala, Ogun, Oshosi, Shango

99. Obara Oyeku, Obara Oyekun, Obara Yeku, Obara Kuye

+

O I

O O

O O

O O

Principle: Self-transformation leads to end of a cycle

Herbs: Almacigo, Itamo Real, Cundiamor, Mangle Prieto

Orisha speaking: Obatala, Oshun, Shango, Yemaya

100. Obara Iwori, Obara Wori, Obara Wereko

+

O I

I O

I O

O O

Principle: Self-transformation leads to transformation

Herbs: San Diego, Palma, Areca, Garro

Orisha speaking: Eshu, Obatala, Orunmila, Yemaya, Egun

101. Obara Odi, Obara Di, Obara Dila

\+

I I

O O

O O

I O

Principle: Self-transformation leads to rebirth

Herbs: Tua Tua, Malambo, Yagruma, Higuereta, Caisimon, Cagadilla de Gallina

Orisha speaking: Orunmila, Eshu, Babaluaye, Osanyin, Shango, Yemaya

102. Obara Irosun, Obara Iroso, Obara Roso, Obara Koso

\+

I I

I O

O O

O O

Principle: Self-transformation leads to fulfillment of creative potential

Herbs: Marana, Tomate, Cimarron, Escoba Amarga, Hierba Lechera, Hierba la Vieja, Ewe Ayo

Orisha speaking: Orunmila, Obatala, Olokun, Babaluaye, Shango, Ibeji, Osun, Eshu, Yemaya

103. Obara Owonrin, Obara Ojuani

+

O I

O O

I O

I O

Principle: Self-transformation creates an unexpected outcome

Herbs: Atori, Guacamaya

Orisha speaking: Olofin, Shango, Orunmila, Eshu, Obatala

104. Obara Okanran, Obara Okana, Obara Kana

+

O I

O O

O O

I O

Principle: Self-transformation leads to a new direction

Herbs: Canistel, Palo Ramon, Algarrobo, Yierba Bruja

Orisha speaking: Shango, Orunmila, Eshu, Oya

105. Obara Ogunda, Obara Gunda

+

I I

I O

I O

O O

Principle: Self-transformation leads to conflict (or removal of obstacles)

Herbs: Flor de Agua, Peonia, Marikape, Calabaza, Ñame

Orisha speaking: Orunmila, Eleda, Elegba, Ogun, Olofin

106. Obara Osa, Obara Sa

+

O I

I O

I O

I O

Principle: Self-transformation creates sudden change

Herbs: Papaya, Erete, Artemisa

Orisha speaking: Olofin, Orunmila, Obatala, Oshun, Agayu, Irawo

107. Obara Ika, Obara Ka

+

OI

IO

OO

OO

Principle: Self-transformation leads to a gathering of Asé

Herbs: Flor de Agua, Yagruma

Orisha speaking: Eleda, Orunmila, Eshu, Ogun, Olofin, Shango, Obatala

108. Obara Oturupon, Obara Otrupon, Obara Trupo

+

O I

O O

I O

O O

Principle: Self-transformation creates good health (or disease)

Herbs: Guara, Caimitillo, Maiz, Calabaza

Orisha speaking: Orunmila, Oya, Ogun, Obatala, Eshu

109. Obara Otura, Obara Tura, Obara Turale, Obara Kushiyo

```
      +
     I I
     O O
     I O
     I O
```

Principle: Self-transformation leads to spiritual consciousness

Herbs: Melon de Castilla, Piñon de Botija, Picuala

Orisha speaking: Orunmila, Eshu, Oshun, Ogun, Obatala, Shango, Egun

110. Obara Irete, Obara Rete

```
      +
     I I
     I O
     O O
     I O
```

Principle: Self-transformation creates determination

Herbs: Canutillo, Iroko, Himo de Oshun, Guiro

Orisha speaking: Orunmila, Olokun, Ogun, Shango, Yemaya, Oshun, Obatala, Inle

111. Obara Ose, Obara Oshe, Obara She

<pre>
       +
      I I
      O O
      I O
      O O
</pre>

Principle: Self-transformation creates fertility

Herbs: Penca de Guano, Guia Blanca

Orisha speaking: Orunmila, Oshun, Eshu, Osanyin, Olofin, Obba

112. Obara Ofun, Obara Fun

<pre>
       +
      O I
      I O
      O O
      I O
</pre>

Principle: Self-transformation leads to a miracle

Herbs: Don Chayo

Orisha speaking: Olofin, Orunmila, Eshu, Egun, Obatala, Inle

113. Baba Okanran Meji, Baba Okana Meyi

+

O O

O O
O O

I I

Principle: Creates a new direction

Herbs: Yantan, Ajonjoli

Orisha speaking: Shango, Ibejis, Oya, Egun, Orunmila, Obatala, Agayu, Babaluaye, Eshu

114. Okanran Ogbe, Okana Ogbe, Okana Sode

+

I O

I O

I O

I I

Principle: A new direction creates an open road

Herbs: Bejuco, Mostacilla, Salvadera

Orisha speaking: Eshu, Oya, Ogun, Oshosi, Olofin, Orunmila, Obatala, Inle Abata, Iku

115. Okanran Oyeku, Okana Oyekun, Okana Yeku

```
        +
       O O
       O O
       O O
       O I
```

Principle: A new direction creates an end to a cycle

Herbs: Aji GuaGuao, Guiro

Orisha speaking: Olodumare, Egun, Eshu, Ogun, Orunmila

116. Okanran Iwori, Okana Iwori

```
        +
       O O
       I O
       I O
       O I
```

Principle: A new direction leads to transformation

Herbs: Aji Picante

Orisha speaking: Eshu, Osanyin, Olofin, Orunmila, Shango

117. Okanran Odi, Okana Odi, Okana Di

+

I O

O O

O O

I I

Principle: A new direction leads to rebirth

Herbs: Vencedor, Vence Batalla

Orisha speaking: Eshu, Orunmila, Yemaya, Shango, Orisha-nla, Ogun, Oshun

118. Okanran Irosun, Okana Iroso, Okana Roso

+

I O

I O

O O

O I

Principle: A new direction leads to fulfillment of creative potential

Herbs: Palo de Lechuga, Atiponla, Escoba Amarga, Huevo de Gallo

Orisha speaking: Shango, Osanyin, Olokun, Orunmila, Eshu, Oshun

119. Okanran Owonrin, Okana Ojuani

+

O O

O O

I O

I I

Principle: A new direction creates an unexpected outcome

Herbs: Hierba Don Carlo, Maloja, Maiz

Orisha speaking: Yalorde, Eshu, Olokun, Ibejis, Osanyin, Egun, Babaluaye, Orunmila

120. Okanran Obara, Okana Obara

+

I O

O O

O O

O I

Principle: A new direction leads to self-transformation

Herbs: Jiqui, Vence Guerra, Ñame

Orisha speaking: Orunmila, Eshu, Shango, Obatala, Oya, Osanyin

121. Okanran Ogunda, Okana Ogunda, Okana Gunda

<pre>
        +
      I O
      I O
      I O
      O I
</pre>

Principle: A new direction leads to conflict (or removal of obstacles)

Herbs: Ewereyeye, Capili, Pomarrosa, Caimito

Orisha speaking: Eshu, Shango, Orunmila, Ogun, Obatala

122. Okanran Osa, Okana Osa, Okana Sa

<pre>
        +
      O O
      I O
      I O
      I I
</pre>

Principle: A new direction creates sudden change

Herbs: Lirio, Cardon, Hojas de Mani, Caguarian

Orisha speaking: Olodumare, Eshu, Shango, Orunmila, Ogun, Oshosi, Obatala

123. Okanran Ika, Okana Ika, Okana Ka

+

O O

I O

O O

O I

Principle: A new direction leads a gathering of Asé

Herbs: Majagua, Bleo Blanco, Bleo Colorado, Estropajo, Guira Amarga

Orisha speaking: Obatala, Olokun, Orunmila, Egun, Eshu, Oshosi, Oshun, Oya

124. Okanran Oturupon, Okana Otrupon, Okana Trupon

+

O O

O O

I O

O I

Principle: A new direction leads to good health (or disease)

Herbs: Maravilla, Pimienta

Orisha speaking: Olodumare, Osanyin, Eshu, Shango, Ayaguna

125. Okanran Otura, Okana Otura, Okana Turale

+

I O

O O

I O

I I

Principle: A new direction leads to spiritual consciousness

Herbs: Guama, Hierba Hedionda, Tua Tua

Orisha speaking: Eshu, Orunmila, Shango, Yemaya

126. Okanran Irete, Okana Irete, Okana Rete

+

I O

I O

O O

I I

Principle: A new direction creates determination

Herbs: Santa Juana, Laurel

Orisha speaking: Obatala, Eshu, Orunmila, Shango, Osanyin, Ogun, Oshun

127. Okanran Ose, Okana Oshe, Okana She

+

I O

O O

I O

O I

Principle: A new direction creates fertility

Herbs: Estropajo, Malvate, Quita Maldicion, Cupido

Orisha speaking: Orunmila, Eshu, Oshun, Shango, Oya

128. Okanran Ofun, Okana Ofun, Okana Fun

+

O O

I O

O O

I I

Principle: A new direction creates a miracle

Herbs: Peonia, Guiro, Majagua, Prodigiosa, Algodon, Ñame

Orisha speaking: Orisha-nla, Egun, Iya, Ogun, Oya, Orunmila, Shango

129. Baba Ogunda Meji, Baba Ogunda Meyi

<pre>
          +
         I I
         I I
         I I
         O O
</pre>

Principle: Creates the removal of obstacles, conflict

Herbs: Malvate, Peregun

Orisha speaking: Orunmila, Ogun, Obatala, Eshu, Oshosi, Shango, Ibejis, Babaluaye, Egun

130. Ogunda Ogbe, Ogunda Bede, Ogunda Biode

<pre>
          +
         I I
         I I
         I I
         I O
</pre>

Principle: Conflict (or removal of obstacles) creates a new road

Herbs: Peregun, Aila, Yanten, Iroko, Chayo, Achibata, Yagruma

Orisha speaking: Orunmila, Osanyin, Oshun, Orisha-Oko, Eshu, Oshumare, Yemaya, Egun

131. Ogunda Oyeku, Ogunda Oyekun, Ogunda Yeku

```
    +
   O I
   O I
   O I
   O O
```

Principle: Conflict (or removal of obstacles) leads to end of a cycle

Herbs: Ciruela

Orisha speaking: Orunmila, Ogun, Osanyin, Babaluaye, Shango, Aleyo

132. Ogunda Iwori, Ogunda Wori

```
    +
   O I
   I I
   I I
   O O
```

Principle Conflict (or removal of obstacles) leads to transformation

Herbs: Verdolaga de Costa, Capullo de Algodon

Orisha speaking: Eshu, Olokun, Shango, Ogun, Yemaya

133. Ogunda Odi, Ogunda Di, Dio

+

I I

O I

O I

I O

Principle: Conflict (or removal of obstacles) leads to rebirth

Herbs: Uña de Gato, Malacara

Orisha speaking: Obatala, Yemaya, Yalorde, Ogun

134. Ogunda Irosun, Ogunda Iroso, Ogunda Roso

+

I I

I I

O I

O O

Principle: Conflict (or removal of obstacles) leads to fulfillment of creative potential

Herbs: Junco Marino, Cabalonga, Canutillo

Orisha speaking: Eshu, Ogun, Osun, Oya, Shango, Orunmila, Oshun, Obatala

135. Ogunda Owonrin, Ogunda Ojuani, Ogunda Leni

+

O I

O I

I I

I O

Principle: Conflict (or removal of obstacles) creates an unexpected outcome

Herbs: Palo Caballero, Amansa Guapo, Vence Batalla

Orisha speaking: Eshu, Ogun, Oshosi, Oya, Orunmila

136. Ogunda Obara, Ogunda Bara

+

I I

O I

O I

O O

Principle Conflict (or removal of obstacles) leads to self-transformation

Herbs: Oreja de Gato, Amor Seco

Orisha speaking: None

137. Ogunda Okanran, Ogunda Okana, Ogunda Kana, Ogunda Ko

+

O I

O I

O I

I O

Principle: Conflict (or removal of obstacles) creates a new direction

Herbs: Caimito, Uva Caleta

Orisha speaking: Olofin, Obatala, Shango, Eshu

138. Ogunda Osa, Ogunda Sa, Ogunda Masa

+

O I

I I

I I

I O

Principle: Conflict (or removal of obstacles) creates sudden change

Herbs: Cobalongo, Palo Caballero

Orisha speaking: Olofin, Ogun, Oshosi, Orunmila, Eshu, Oshun

139. Ogunda Ika, Ogunda Ka

+

O I

I I

O I

O O

Principle: Conflict (or removal of obstacles) leads to a gathering of Asé

Herbs: Algodon, Salvia

Orisha speaking: Orunmila, Ogun, Eshu

140. Ogunda Oturupon, Ogunda Otrupon, Ogunda Trupo

+

O I

O I

I I

O O

Principle: Conflict (or removal of obstacles) creates good health (or disease)

Herbs: Granada, Almacigo, Acacia, Flor de Agua

Orisha speaking: Eshu, Orunmila, Ogun, Babaluaye, Iya

141. Ogunda Otura, Ogunda Tetura

<pre>
      +
     I I
     O I
     I I
     I O
</pre>

Principle Conflict (or removal of obstacles) creates spiritual consciousness

Herbs: Guasima, Curujey, Jobo, Ceiba, Salvadera, Jala Jala

Orisha speaking: Orunmila, Osanyin, Shango, Oshun, Obatala, Ogun

142. Ogunda Irete, Ogunda Kete

<pre>
      +
     I I
     I I
     O I
     I O
</pre>

Principle: Conflict (or removal of obstacles) creates determination

Herbs: Romerillo, Guira, Ayua, Ñame

Orisha speaking: Orunmila, Osanyin, Ogun, Obatala, Iya, Oshun, Elegba

143. Ogunda Ose, Ogunda Oshe, Ogunda She

+

I I

O I

I I

O O

Principle: Conflict (or removal of obstacles) creates fertility

Herbs: Paraiso, Alacrancillo, Escoba Amarga, Cundiamor, Roble, Cuye Cuye, Peonia

Orisha speaking: Olofin, Orunmila, Yalorde, Ogun, Eshu, Babaluaye, Shango, Oya

144. Ogunda Ofun, Ogunda Fun

+

O I

I I

O I

I O

Principle: Conflict (or removal of obstacles) creates a miracle

Herbs: Prodijiosa, Tamarindo, Atori, Ewe Ikoko, Ewe Ayo, Bugandil

Orisha speaking: Orunmila, Oshun, Elegba, Ogun, Oshosi

145. Baba Osa Meji, Baba Osa Meyi

```
      +
     O O
     I I
     I I
     I I
```

Principle: Creates sudden change

Herbs: Jasmine, Algodon

Orisha speaking: Obatala, Oke, Shango, Eshu, Orunmila, Ajes, Ogun, Osanyin, Babaluaye, Egun

146. Osa Ogbe, Osalofogbeyo

```
      +
     I O
     I I
     I I
     I I
```

Principle: Sudden change creates an open road

Herbs: Acelga, Espanta Muerto, Plantano, Escoba Amarga, Cambia Voz, Dominador

Orisha speaking: Eshu, Shango, Babaluaye, Obatala, Olofin, Orunmila, Yemaya, Oshun

147. Osa Oyeku, Osa Oyekun, Osa Yeku

+

O O

O I

O I

O I

Principle: Sudden change creates end of a cycle

Herbs: Albahaca Morada, Vinagrillo

Orisha speaking: Orisha-Oko, Shango, Oshun, Ibejis

148. Osa Iwori, Osa Wori, Osa Wo

+

O O

I I

I I

O I

Principle: Sudden change leads to transformation

Herbs: Almendra, Bayadona, Agracejo

Orisha speaking: Eshu, Shango, Orisha-Oko, Agayu, Oshun, Orunmila, Egun

149. Osa Odi, Osa Di

+

I O

O I

O I

I I

Principle: Sudden change creates rebirth

Herbs: Helecho Macho, Mejorana

Orisha speaking: Osun, Yemaya, Eshu, Orunmila, Oshun, Obatala

150. Osa Irosun, Osa Iroso, Osa Roso

+

I O

I I

O I

O I

Principle: Sudden change leads to fulfillment of creative potential

Herbs: Alamo, Hierba Buena, Ceremi

Orisha speaking: Shango, Orunmila, Babaluaye, Obatala

151. Osa Owonrin, Osa Ojuani, Osa Loni

+

O O

O I

I I

I I

Principle: Sudden change creates an unexpected outcome

Herbs: Cedro, Palma de Coco

Orisha speaking: Olofin, Obatala, Eshu, Oke, Oshun, Babaluaye, Shango, Osanyin

152. Osa Obara, Osa Bara, Osa Shepe

+

I O

O I

O I

O I

Principle: Sudden change leads to self-transformation

Herbs: Zarzapilla, Ceiba, Algodon, Prodijiosa

Orisha speaking: Orunmila, Yemeya, Obatala, Ala, Shango, Oya

153. Osa Okanran, Osa Okana, Osa kana

+

O O

O I

O I

I I

Principle: Sudden change creates a new direction

Herbs: Aroma, Caimito, Tamarindo, Jiqui, Jeguey, Bleo Blanco, Amansa Guapo, Ceiba, Atiponla, Salvia, Cambia Voz

Orisha speaking: Olokun, Shango, Oya, Yemaya, Obatala, Orunmila, Eleda, Ala

154. Osa Ogunda, Osa Gunda, Osa Guleya

+

I O

I I

I I

O I

Principle: Sudden change leads to conflict (or removal of obstacles)

Herbs: Curujey, Jeguey, Araba, Leguelo

Orisha speaking: Olofin, Shango, Osanyin, Eshu, Oya, Obatala, Ogun

155. Osa Ika, Osa Ka

+

O O

I I

O I

O I

Principle: Sudden change leads to a gathering of Asé

Herbs: Jia Amarilla, Manto, Culantrillo

Orisha speaking: Orunmila, Egun, Ogun

156. Osa Oturupon, Osa Otrupon, Osa Trupo

+

O O

O I

I I

O I

Principle: Sudden change creates good health (or disease)

Herbs: Guasima

Orisha speaking: Orunmila, Oke, Shango, Yalorde, Obatala, Ala Iya

157. Osa Otura, Osa Tura, Osaure

+

I O

O I

I I

I I

Principle: Sudden change leads to spiritual consciousness

Herbs: Plantanom Sauco Blanco, Perejil y Hierba de la Costa

Orisha speaking: Eshu, Obatala, Olokun, Oya, Osun, Babaluaye, Oshun, Osanyin, Egun

158. Osa Irete, Osa Rete

+

I O

I I

O I

I I

Principle: Sudden change creates determination

Herbs: Hierba Hedionda (Gunina), Yaya, Hierba Cano

Orisha speaking: Obatala, Shango, Orunmila, Eshu, Igba Iwa Odu, Olokun, Iya

159. Osa Ose, Osa Oshe, Osa She

+

I O

O I

I I

O I

Principle: Sudden change creates fertility

Herbs: Flor de Agua, Pico de Pato, Zangazo

Orisha speaking: Olokun, Orunmila, Yemaya, Obatala, Eleggua, Shango, Oshun, Obirin

160. Osa Ofun, Osa Fun

+

O O

I I

O I

I I

Principle: Sudden change creates a miracle

Herbs: Atiponla, Prodijiosa, Ruda Cimarrona

Orisha speaking: Obatala, Oya, Eshu, Olofin, Osanyin

161. Baba Ika Meji, Baba Ika Meyi

+

O O

I I

O O

O O

Principle: Creates a gathering of Asé

Herbs: Ewe oriye, Cerraja

Orisha speaking: Orunmila, Ogun, Yemaya, Ori, Osanyin, Oduduwa, Eshu, Oshosi, Ona

162. Ika Ogbe

+

I O

I I

I O

I O

Principle: A gathering of Asé creates an open road

Herbs: Anacaguita, Graba, Beria, No me Olvides

Orisha speaking: Eshu, Elegba, Orunmila, Yemaya

163. Ika Oyeku, Ika Oyekun, Ika Yeku

+

O O

O I

O O

O O

Principle: A gathering of Asé creates the end of a cycle

Herbs: Guacalote, Salvia, Tuya

Orisha speaking: Orunmila, Shango, Babaluaye, Yemaya, Eshu, Ibejis, Orisha-Oko, Iku

164. Ika Iwori, Ika Wori

+

O O

I I

I O

O O

Principle: A gathering of Asé leads to transformation

Herbs: Abaro, Ocidiana

Orisha speaking: Eshu, Olofin, Yemaya, Orunmila, Oshun, Osanyin

165. Ika Odi, Ika Di

\+

I O

O I

O O

I O

Principle: A gathering of Asé creates rebirth

Herbs: Colonia, Panetela, Orozus, Canela, Vervena

Orisha speaking: Orunmila, Eshu, Obatala, Shango

166. Ika Irosun, Ika Iroso, Ika Roso

\+

I O

I I

O O

O O

Principle: A gathering of Asé leads to fulfillment of creative potential

Herbs: Alacrancillo, Algarrobo, Anacaguita, Copey, Mango Macho

Orisha speaking: Osun, Olofin, Eshu, Osanyin, Shango, Yemaya

167. Ika Owonrin, Ika Ojuani, Ika Juani

+

O O

O I

I O

I O

Principle: A gathering of Asé creates an unexpected outcome

Herbs: Clavellina, Rosa, Francesa, Palo Bomba

Orisha speaking: Yemeya, Oshun, Orunmila, Eshu, Osanyin, Obatala

168. Ika Obara, Ika Bara

+

I O

O I

O O

O O

Principle: A gathering of Asé leads to self-transformation

Herbs: Pega Pollo

Orisha speaking: Eshu, Orunmila, Obatala, Olokun

169. Ika Okanran, Ika Okana, Ika Kana

+

O O

O I

O O

I O

Principle: A gathering of Asé creates a new direction

Herbs: Bejuco Tortuga, Palo Jicotea

Orisha speaking: Obatala, Oshun, Egun, Ogun

170. Ika Ogunda, Ika Gunda

+

I O

I I

I O

O O

Principle: A gathering of Asé creates conflict (or removal of obstacles)

Herbs: Bejuco Lechero

Orisha speaking: Orunmila, Ogun, Osanyin, Yemaya, Inle, Eshu, Olofin

171. Ika Osa, Ika Sa

```
      +
     O O
     I I
     I O
     I O
```

Principle: A gathering of Asé creates sudden change

Herbs: Algarrabo, Alamo

Orisha speaking: Orunmila, Oya, Obatala, Ogun

172. Ika Oturupon, Ika Otrupon, Ika Trupon

```
      +
     O O
     O I
     I O
     O O
```

Principle: A gathering of Asé creates good health (or disease)

Herbs: Yagruma, Jaguey

Orisha speaking: Orunmila, Oya, Shango, Yemaya, Eshu

173. Ika Otura, Ika Tura, Ika Foguero

+

I O

O I

I O

I O

Principle: A gathering of Asé leads to spiritual consciousness

Herbs: Jeranico Rojo, Girasol

Orisha speaking: Olorun, Ala, Oya, Obatala, Orunmila, Oshun

174. Ika Irete, Ika Rete

+

I O

I I

O O

I O

Principle: A gathering of Asé creates determination

Herbs: Himo de Oshun, Uva Caleta, Uva Gomos, Acacia

Orisha speaking: Orunmila, Eshu, Yemaya, Ogun, Shango, Oshun, Olofin, Olokun

175. Ika Ose, Ika Oshe, Ika She

+

I O

O I

I O

O O

Principle: A gathering of Asé creates fertility

Herbs: Pata Gallina, Algodon, Vergonzosa, Granada, Gresella

Orisha speaking: Orunmila, Eshu, Obatala, Oshun, Ogun

176. Ika Ofun, Ika Fun

+

O O

I I

O O

I O

Principle: A gathering of Asé creates a miracle

Herbs: Guabico, Guairaje, Prodijiosa, Azucena, Flor de Aroma

Orisha speaking: Orunmila, Eshu, Obatala, Ibejis, Shango, Ogun, Oya, Osanyin

177. Baba Oturupon Meji, Baba Otrupon Meyi

+

O O

O O

I I

O O

Principle: Creates maintenance of health

Herbs: Salvia, Retama

Orisha speaking: Elegba, Ogun, Orunmila, Obatala, Egungun, Oya, Ile, Odu, Oke, Babaluaye

178. Oturupon Ogbe, Otrupon Ogbe, Otrupon Bekonwa

+

I O

I O

I I

I O

Principle: Maintenance of health to an open road

Herbs: Canistel, Palo Tambor, Encedro, Lengua de Vaca, Cedro

Orisha speaking: Shango, Eshu, Olofin, Ogun, Orunmila

179. Oturupon Oyeku, Otrupon Oyekun, Otrupon Yeku

+

O O

O O

O I

O O

Principle: Good Maintenance of health creates the end of a cycle

Herbs: Mani, Cascabelillo, Curujey

Orisha speaking: Eshu, Obatala, Shango, Ogun, Ibejis, Orisha-Oko

180. Oturupon Iwori, Otrupon Iwori, Otrupon Adakino

+

O O

I O

I I

O O

Principle: Maintenance of health leads to transformation

Herbs: Algarrabo, Cascarapita y Cacaya

Orisha speaking: Oya, Oro, Egun, Iku, Eleggua, Orunmila, Oshun, Obatala, Shango, Ogun

181. Oturupon Odi, Otrupon Odi

+

I O

O O

O I

I O

Principle: Maintenance of health leads to rebirth

Herbs: Carquesa, Sacu Sacu, Maiz

Orisha speaking: Ogun, Shango, Orunmila, Osanyin, Eshu

182. Oturupon Irosun, Otrupon Iroso, Otrupon Koso

+

I O

I O

O I

OO

Principle: Maintenance of health leads to fulfillment of creative potential

Herbs: Palo Moro, Retama, Palo Malambo

Orisha speaking: Eshu, Orunmila, Shango, Babaluaye, Obatala, Ogun

183. Oturupon Owonrin, Otrupon Ojuani

+

O O

O O

I I

I O

Principle: Maintenance of health creates an unexpected outcome

Herbs: Reseda, Roble, Dagame

Orisha speaking: Orunmila, Eshu, Oya, Ogun, Egun, Olokun

184. Oturupon Obara, Otrupon Obara, Otrupon Baraife

+

I O

O O

O I

O O

Principle: Maintenance of health leads to self-transformation

Herbs: Orisha-Oko, Shango, Orunmila, Ogun, Elegba, Olokun

Orisha speaking: Orisha-Oko, Shango, Orunmila, Ogun, Oshun, Elegba, Olokun

185. Oturupon Okanran, Otrupon Okana, Otrupon Kana

+

O O

O O

O I

I O

Principle: Maintenance of health leads to a new direction

Herbs: Maravilla

Orisha speaking: Orunmila, Eshu, Ogun, Babalawo

186. Oturupon Ogunda, Otrupon Ogunda, Otrupon Gunda

+

I O

I O

I I

O O

Principle: Maintenance of health creates conflict (or removal of obstacles)

Herbs: Guiro, Malvira, Malva Blanca

Orisha speaking: Orunmila, Shango, Oshun, Yemaya, Eshu, Ogun, Obatala, Osanyin

187. Oturupon Osa, Otrupon Osa, Otrupon Sa

+

O O

I O

I I

I O

Principle: Maintenance of health creates sudden change

Herbs: Mastuerzo, Manzanilla

Orisha speaking: Orunmila, Eshu, Egun, Ogun, Shango

188. Oturupon Ika, Otrupon Ika, Otrupon Ka

+

O O

I O

O I

O O

Principle; Maintenance of health leads to a gathering of Asé

Herbs: Salvia, Retama

Orisha speaking: Shango, Obatala, Oshun, Eshu, Orunmila, Asojuano, Ogun, Oduduwa, Osanyin, Ibejis, Nanu

189. Oturupon Otura, Otrupon Otura, Otrupon Tauro

+

I O

O O

I I

I O

Principle: Maintenance of health creates manifestation of prayer

Herbs: Mije, Mejorana

Orisha speaking: Obatala, Shango, Orunmila

190. Oturupon Irete, Otrupon Irete

+

I O

I O

O I

I O

Principle: Maintenance of health creates determination

Herbs: Canutillo, Verdolaga, Tomate

Orisha speaking: Orunmila, Osanyin, Eshu, Shango, Obatala, Oshosi, Olokun

191. Oturupon Ose, Otrupon Oshe, Otrupon She

+

I O

O O

I I

O O

Principle: Maintenance of health creates fertility

Herbs: Parami, Cedro, Aroma, Amanza Guapo, Ayua

Orisha speaking: Shango, Oshun, Orunmila, Eshu, Obatala

192. Oturupon Ofun, Otrupon Ofun, Otrupon Fun

+

O O

I O

O I

I O

Principle: Maintenance of health creates a miracle

Herbs: Apazote, Okuje, Mil Flores

Orisha speaking: Eleda, Obatala, Osun, Orunmila, Eshu, Egun

193. Baba Otura Meji, Baba Otura Meyi

<pre>
          +
          I I
          O O
          I I
          I I
</pre>

Principle: Creates spiritual consciousness

Herbs: Acacia, Trebol

Orisha speaking: Eshu, Olofin, Orunmila, Shango, Oduduwa, Oshun, Ogun, Oshosi, Babaluaye

194. Otura Ogbe, Otura Niko

<pre>
          +
          I I
          I O
          I I
          I I
</pre>

Principle: Spiritual consciousness creates an open road

Herbs: Curujey, Caimito, Ashibata, Ateje, Rabo de Gato

Orisha speaking: Orunmila, Eshu, Egun, Shango, Oya, Oshun

195. Otura Oyeku, Otura Oyekun, Otura Yeku

+

O I

O O

O I

O I

Principle: Spiritual consciousness creates an end of a cycle

Herbs: Ikoko

Orisha speaking: Eshu, Abita, Orunmila, Obatala, Babaluaye, Oduduwa, Olofin

196. Otura Iwori, Otura Wori, Otura Pompeyo

+

O I

I O

I I

O I

Principle: Spiritual consciousness leads to transformation

Herbs: Guacalote, Alacrancillo

Orisha speaking: Orunmila, Eshu, Olokun, Orisha-nla

197. Otura Odi, Otura Di, Otura Diablo

+

I I

O O

O I

I I

Principle: Spiritual consciousness creates rebirth

Herbs: Mamey, Mamoncillo

Orisha speaking: Ibejis, Orunmila, Obatala, Shango, Oshun, Olodumare, Yemaya

198. Otura Irosun, Otura Iroso

+

I I

I O

O I

O I

Principle: Spiritual consciousness leads to fulfillment of creative potential

Herbs: Ceiba, Igi Egungun, Ikoko, Majagua, Palma, Yarey Ope, Mamoncillo, Guanina Lode

Orisha speaking: Yewa, Iroko, Egungun, Apa, Orunmila, Oshun, Shango, Ogun

199. Otura Owonrin, Otura Ojuani

+

O I

O O

I I

I I

Principle: Spiritual consciousness leads to an unexpected outome

Herbs: Prodigiosa, Tete, Nene, Laurel, Ateje

Orisha speaking: Olodumare, Eshu, Obatala, Orunmila, Yalorde, Shango, Osanyin

200. Otura Obara, Otura Bara

+

I I

O O

O I

O I

Principle: Spiritual consciousness leads to self-transformation

Herbs: Meloncillo, Majagua, Abre Camino, Hiedra, Ceiba, Tamarindo, Melon de Castilla

Orisha speaking: Osanyin, Eshu, Aiye, Oya, Shango, Babaluaye, Obatala, Orunmila, Oshun, Osun, Awo

201. Otura Okanran, Otura Okana, Otura Kana, Otura Tiku

+

O I

O O

O I

I I

Principle: Spiritual consciousness creates a new direction

Herbs: Paraiso, Salvia, Canutillo, Aberincunlo, Algarrobo, Romerillo, Albahaca, Quita Maldicion

Orisha speaking: Orunmila, Yanza, Shango, Yemaya, Ogun, Oshosi, Babaluaye, Obatala

202. Otura Ogunda, Otura Gunda, Otura Aira

+

I I

I O

I I

O I

Principle: Spiritual consciousness leads to conflict (or removal of obstacles)

Herbs: Mirra

Orisha speaking: Olofin, Orunmila, Ogun, Osanyin, Obatala, Eshu, Shango, Yemaya, Olokun

203. Otura Osa, Otura Sa

+

O I

I O

I I

I I

Principle: Spiritual consciousness creates sudden change

Herbs: Guacamaya, Caisimon

Orisha speaking: Orunmila, Eshu, Obatala, Olofin, Shango, Oya

204. Otura Ika, Otura ka

+

O I

I O

O I

O I

Principle: Spiritual consciousness leads to a gathering of Asé

Herbs: Taboni, Dormidera, Algodon

Orisha speaking: Obatala, Olofin, Orunmila, Ogun, Eshu

205. Otura Oturupon, Otura Otrupon, Otura Trupon

\+

O I

O O

I I

O I

Principle: Spiritual consciousness creates good health (or disease)

Herbs: Abre Camino, Paraiso Frances

Orisha speaking: Orunmila, Olofin, Shango, Eshu, Oshosi, Olokun, Ogun, Yemaya

206. Otura Irete

\+

I I

I O

O I

I I

Principle: Spiritual consciousness creates determination

Herbs: Flamboyan, Platano, Caisimon, Espartillo, Datil

Orisha speaking: Olofin, Orisha, Eshu, Ogun, Oshosi, Orunmila, Ibejis

207. Otura Ose, Otura Oshe, Otura Oshe

+

I I

O O

I I

O I

Principle: Spiritual consciousness leads to spiritual consciousness

Herbs: Verdolaga Francesa, Ñame

Orisha speaking: Obatala, Elegba, Ibejis, Egun

208. Otura Ofun, Otura Fun, Otura Adakoy

+

O I

I O

O I

I I

Principle: Spiritual consciousness creates a miracle

Herbs: Ewe oriye, Salvia, Aberincunlo, Quita Maldicion, Diez del Dia

Orisha speaking: Ogun, Oshun, Yemaya, Iku, Obatala, Orunmila, Shango

209. Baba Irete Meji, Baba Irete Meyi

+

I I

I I

O O

I I

Principle: Creates determination

Herbs: Pensamiento, Ewewa

Orisha speaking: Odus of Ifa, Orunmila, Babaluaye, Eshu, Oshun, Shango, Oramfe, Oro, Oshosi

210. Irete Ogbe, Irete Untelu, Irete Entebe More

+

I I

I I

I O

I I

Principle: Determination creates an open road

Herbs: Bleo Colorado, Bleo Blanco, Pata Gallina, Verdolaga, Cundiamor, Ciruela

Orisha speaking: Orunmila, Osanyin, Obatala, Olofin, Shango, Oshosi, Ogun, Eshu

211. Irete Oyeku, Irete Oyekun, Irete Yeku, Irete Yerube

+

O I

O I

O O

O I

Principle: Determination leads to end of a cycle

Herbs: Zarazparilla, Alacrana

Orisha speaking: Eshu, Shango, Yalorde, Orunmila, Ogun

212. Irete Iwori, Irete Yero

+

O I

I I

I O

O I

Principle: Determination leads to transformation

Herbs: Orosus, Boton de Oro, Rompe Saraguey, Quital Maldicion, Bleo Blanco

Orisha speaking: Orunmila, Osanyin, Oro, Egun Obinisa, Yalorde, Eshu, Olodumare, Gunugun

213. Irete Odi, Irete Di, Irete Untedi

+

I I

O I

O O

I I

Principle: Determination leads to rebirth

Herbs: Doradilla, Vicaria Blanca

Orisha speaking: Sjango, Orunmila, Osanyin, Eshu, Oshun, Ogun, Olofin, Yemaya

214. Irete Irosun, Irete Iroso, Irete Roso, Irete Lazo

+

I I

I I

O O

O I

Principle: Determination leads to fulfillment of creative potential

Herbs: Salvia, Moruro, Yerba Bruja, Peonia

Orisha speaking: Orunmila, Eshu, Shango, Yalorde, Omo

215. Irete Owonrin, Irete Ojuani, Irete Juani, Irete Wan Wan

+

O I

O I

I O

I I

Principle: Determination leads to an unexpected outcome

Herbs: Higo, Platano, Lino deRio, Ajonjoli

Orisha speaking: Osanyin, Obatala, Oshun, Eshu, Babaluaye, Orunmila, Irunmoles

216. Irete Obara, Irete Bara, Irete Oba

+

I I

O I

O O

O I

Principle: Determination leads to self-transformation

Herbs: Ewefa, Bejuco Garanon, Pendejera

Orisha speaking: Shango, Obatala, Yemaya, Oya, Yalorde, Orunmila, Obirin

217. Irete Okanran, Irete Okana, Irete Kana

+

O I

OI

O O

I I

Principle: Determination leads to a new direction

Herbs: Tamarindo, Raiz de Coco, Fruta Bomba, Ikoko, Ijagua

Orisha speaking: Olofin, Obatala, Orunmila, Eshu

218. Irete Ogunda, Irete Gunda, Irete Kutan, Irete Keda

+

I I

I I

I O

O I

Principle: Determination leads to conflict (or removal of obstacles)

Herbs: Acelga, Verdolaga, Juacaro, Guama, Algarrobo, Guacamaya, Jobo, Itamo Real

Orisha speaking: Obatala, Orunmila, Ogun, Oshosi, Oshun, Yemaya, Inle Oguere

219. Irete Osa, Irete Sa, Irete Ansa, Irete Tomusa

```
      +
     O I
     I I
     I O
     I I
```

Principle: Determination creates sudden change

Herbs: Manju, Yeren

Orisha speaking: Orunmila, Obatala, Eshu, Shango, Oshun

220. Irete Ika, Irete Ka

```
      +
     O I
     I I
     O O
     O I
```

Principle: Determination leads to a gathering of Asé

Herbs: Pendejera

Orisha speaking: Eshu, Orunmila, Ogun

221. Irete Oturupon, Irete Otrupon, Irete Trupon

```
        +
       O I
       O I
       I O
       O I
```

Principle: Determination leads to good health (or disease)

Herbs: Aila, Mani, Almendra, Tomate, Berenjena, Tete, Ashi Bata, Oyouro, Berbena

Orisha speaking: Eshu, Orunmila, Shango, Yemaya

222. Irete Otura, Irete Tura, Irete Suka

```
        +
       I I
       O I
       I O
       I I
```

Principle: Determination creates spiritual consciousness

Herbs: Don Chayo, Aberincunlo, Jaguey Macho, Guamo, Palma, Aroma

Orisha speaking: Orunmila, Eshu, Oshosi, Oshun, Obatala

223. Irete Ose, Irete Oshe, Irete She, Irete Unfa

+

I I

O I

I O

O I

Principle: Determination creates fertility

Herbs:Canutillo, Prodijiosa, Eucalipto, Tabano

Orisha speaking: Eshu, Orunmila, Babaluaye, Obirin, Oshun

224. Irete Ofun

+

O I

I I

O O

I I

Principle: Determination creates a miracle

Herbs: Jazmin de Cabo, Almasigo

Orisha speaking: Shango, Orunmila, Eshu, Iya, Aganyu

225. Baba Ose Meji, Baba Oshe Meyi

+

I I

O O

I I

O O

Principle: Creates fertility, abundance

Herbs: Palo Pimienta, Orquidia, Tulipan, Curujey

Orisha speaking: Orunmila, Eshu, Oshun, Oro, Osanyin, Babaluaye, Eleda, Ogo

226. Ose Ogbe, Oshe Ogbe, Oshe Nilogbe

+

I I

I O

I I

I O

Principle: Fertility creates an open road

Herbs: Rabo de Zorra, Hierba Pajon

Orisha speaking: Olokun, Olofin, Orunmila, Agemo

227. Ose Oyeku, Oshe Yekun, Oshe Yeku

+

O I

O O

O I

O O

Principle: Fertility creates end of cycle

Herbs: Slavadera, Abrojo, Malva Blanca

Orisha speaking: Oshun, Orunmila, Yemaya, Yewa, Obatala, Eshu, Osanyin

228. Ose Iwori, Oshe Iwori, Oshe Wori, Oshe Paure

+

O I

I O

I I

O O

Principle: Fertility leads to transformation

Herbs: Girasol, Maloja, Clavellina, Curujey

Orisha speaking: Orunmila, Olofin, Oshun, Eshu, Yemaya, Shango, Orun, Egun, Obatala

229. Ose Odi, Oshe Odi, Oshe Di

+

I I

O O

O I

I O

Principle: Fertility leads to rebirth

Herbs: Vencedor

Orisha speaking: Orunmila, Oshun, Eshu, Osanyin, Shango, Ogun, Obirin

230. Ose Irosun, Oshe Iroso, Oshe Roso, Oshe Leso

+

I I

I O

O I

O O

Principle: Fertility leads to fulfillment of creative potential

Herbs: Abrojo, Iroko, Cuaba, Jenjibere, Zarza, Ewe Ayo, Verdolaga, Francesca

Orisha speaking: Eshu, Yalorde, Ogun, Orunmila, Shango, Olorun

231. Ose Owonrin, Oshe Ojuani, Oshe Juani, Oshe Niwe, Oshe Niwo

+

O I

O O

I I

I O

Principle: Fertility creates an unexpected outcome

Herbs: Algarrobo, Oju Gutan, Ewefa, Bledo Blanco

Orisha speaking: Osanyin, Orunmila, Oshun, Olokun, Olofin, Aroni, Ogun, Eshu, Obatala

232. Ose Obara, Oshe Obara, Oshe Bara

+

I I

O O

O I

O O

Principle: Fertility creates self-transformation

Herbs: Raspa Lengua, Laguela

Orisha speaking: Osanyin, Shango, Eshu, Orunmila, Obatala

233. Ose Okanran, Oshe Okana, Oshe Kana, Oshe Folokana, Oshe Karan

+

O I

O O

O I

I O

Principle: Fertility create a new direction

Herbs: Flor Azul, Eteje, Fruta de Pan

Orisha speaking: Eshu, Yalorde, Orunmila, Osanyin, Obatala, Olodumare

234. Ose Ogunda, Oshe Ogunda, Oshe Gunda, Oshe Omolu

+

I I

I O

I I

O O

Principle: Fertility leads to conflict (or removal of obstacles)

Herbs: Prodijiosa, Palo Rompe Hueso, Atori, Cerraja, Mal Pacifico

Orisha speaking: Orunmila, Eshu, Irunmoles

235. Ose Osa, Oshe Osa, Oshe Sa

+

O I

I O

I I

I O

Principle: Fertility creates sudden change

Herbs: Alamo, Varita San Joes, Hierba Pascua

Orisha speaking: Eshu, Shango, Oshun, Ogun, Orunmila, Obatala, Babaluaye

236. Ose Ika, Oshe Ika, Oshe Ka, Oshe Karaka

+

O I

I O

O I

O O

Principle: Fertility creates a gathering of Asé

Herbs: Pata Gallina, Guisazo, Ebano Carbonero

Orisha speaking: Oshun, Orunmila, Eshu, Obatala, Eleda

237. Ose Oturupon, Oshe Otrupon, Oshe Trupon

+

O I

O O

I I

O O

Principle: Fertility leads to good health (or disease)

Herbs: Hierba de la Sangre

Orisha speaking: Eshu, Orunmila, Shango, Egun, Obatala

238. Ose Otura, Oshe Otura, Oshe Tura

+

I I

O O

I I

I O

Principle: Fertility creates spiritual consciousness

Herbs: Mango, Hierba Mora, Sargazo, Moruro, Dagame

Orisha speaking: Orunmila, Olofin, Eshu, Iroko, Oshun, Egun, Ogun

239. Ose Irete, Oshe Irete, Oshe Rete, Oshe Bile

+

I I

I O

O I

I O

Principle: Fertility creates determination

Herbs: Canistel, Filigrama, Coco

Orisha speaking: Orunmila, Eshu, Shango, Oshun, Babalawo, Ogun, Obba, Obatala, Egun

240. Ose Ofun, Oshe Ofun, Oshe Fun

+

O I

I O

O I

I O

Principle: Fertilty creates a miracle

Herbs: Cordovan, Ponasi

Orisha speaking: Orunmila, Obatala, Oshun, Osun, Iku, Aleyo, Yewa, Eshu, Ogun, Shango

241. Baba Ofun Meji, Baba Ofun Meyi, Baba Oragun

+

O O

I I

O O

I I

Principle: Creates a miracle

Herbs: Jazmin, Sandalo, Levantate, Bleo Blanco, Verdolaga, Prodigiosa, Aguedita

Orisha speaking: Odus of Ifa, Oduduwa, Obatala, Eshu, Babaluaye, Ogun, Irunmoles, Iku

242. Ofun Ogbe, Ofun Nalbe

+

I O

I I

I O

I I

Principle: A miracle creates an open road

Herbs: Tua Tua, Paraguita, Quita Maldicion, Guacalote, Peregun, Atiponla, Cipres

Orisha speaking: Orunmila, Eshu, Obatala, Oshun, Egun, Oya

243. Ofun Oyeku, Ofun Oyekun, Ofun Yeku, Ofun Yemilo

+

O O

O I

O O

O I

Principle: A miracle ends a cycle

Herbs: Mani, Pata Gallina, Zazafran, Salvia, Mango Macho

Orisha speaking: Olofin, Obatala, Orunmila, Eshu, Oya, Iku, Egun

244. Ofun Iwori, Ofun Wori, Ofun Gando

+

O O

I I

I O

O I

Principle: A miracle leads to transformation

Herbs: Melon, Frijol, Caballero, Albahaca

Orisha speaking: Shango, Olofin, Orunmila, Eshu, Egun, Odus, Obatala

245. Ofun Odi, Ofun Di

+

I O

O I

O O

I I

Principle: A miracle leads to rebirth

Herbs: Uvas Banosa, Culantrillo de Pozo

Orisha speaking : Eshu, Orunmila

246. Ofun Irosun, Ofun Iroso, Ofun Roso, Ofun Koso, Ofun Biroso

+

I O

I I

O O

O I

Principle: A miracle leads to fulfillment of creative potential

Herbs: Orosus, Zapote

Orisha speaking: Obatala, Olofin, Eshu, Orunmila, Babaluaye, Shango, Oshun, Osun

247. Ofun Owonrin, Ofun Ojuani, Ofun Juani

```
        +
       O O
       O I
       I O
       I I
```

Principle: A miracle creates an unexpected outcome

Herbs: Almasigo, Aguacate

Orisha speaking: Eshu, Obatala, Orunmila, Obatala, Ibejis

248. Ofun Obara, Ofun Bara

```
        +
       I O
       O I
       O O
       O I
```

Principle: A miracle leads to self-transformation

Herbs: Melon, Juan Libre, Baboseo, Aridan

Orisha speaking: Orunmila, Eshu, Olofin, Oya, Obatala, Ogun

249. Ofun Okanran, Ofun Okana, Ofun Kana

```
      +
     O O
     O I
     O O
     I I
```

Principle: A miracle creates a new direction

Herbs: Alamo, Algarrobo, Parquia, Bala de Canon

Orisha speaking: Obatala, Eshu, Osanyin, Orunmila, Shango

250. Ofun Ogunda, Ofun Guna, Ofun Funda

```
      +
     I O
     I I
     I O
     O I
```

Principle: A miracle leads to conflict (or removal of obstacles)

Herbs: Ciruela, Guira, Caranaguey, Bejuco Prieto, Peregun

Orisha speaking: Orunmila, Osanyin, Shango, Obatala, Ogun, Oshun, Babaluaye, Ibejis, Orisha-Oko

251. Ofun Osa, Ofun Sa

+

O O

I I

I O

I I

Principle: A miracle creates sudden change

Herbs : Quita Maldicion, Rompe Camisa, Tate Quieto, Palo Ramon

Orisha speaking: Obatala, Orunmila, Eshu, Osanyin, Iku, Olofin, Olodumare, Oya

252. Ofun Ika

+

O O

I I

O O

O I

Principle: A miracle creates a new direction

Herbs: Cedro, Cuaba Blanca, Ebano Carbonero

Orisha speaking: Eshu, Orunmila, Babaluaye, Obatala

253. Ofun Oturupon, Ofun Otrupon, Ofun Trupon

+

O O

O I

I O

O I

Principle: A miracle creates good health (or disease)

Herbs: Canutillo, Frescura, Escoba Amarga, Albahaca, Morada

Orisha speaking: Oshun, Obatala, Eshu, Orunmila

254. Ofun Otura, Ofun Tura, Ofun Tempola

+

I O

O I

I O

I I

Principle: A miracle leads to spiritual consciousness

Herbs: Zazafra, Ponasi

Orisha speaking: Shango, Eshu, Orunmila, Oshosi

255. Ofun Irete, Ofun Bile

+

I O

I I

O O

I I

Principle: A miracle creates determination

Herbs: Canistel, Filigrama

Orisha speaking: Olofin, Shango, Orunmila, Eshu, Oya, Oshun

256. Ofun Ose, Ofun Oshe, Ofun She

+

I O

O I

I O

O I

Principle: A miracle creates fertility

Herbs: Granada, Clavelina

Orisha speaking: Oshun, Obatala, Orunmila, Eshu, All Souls

Chapter 2

List of Major Orishas

Orisha can be translated to mean "selected head". This is a reference to Orishas as a selected consciousness of the Collective Divine Consciousness.

Ori: One's own head; One's Higher Self

Olodumare: The Creator Consciousness. Olodumare manifests as three consciousnesses: Obatala, Orunmila, and Oduduwa.

Obatala: Omnipresence. Owner of the White Cloth. The Source of Consciousness in Creation.

Orunmila: Omniscience. Witness to Creation. Witness to All Destinies.

Oduduwa: Omnipotence. Power of the Womb. Owner of the Black Womb.

Olokun-Olorun-Onile/Triple Consciousness of the World We Live In: **Olokun**: Owner of the Sea; **Olorun**: Owner of Heaven; **Onile**: Owner of the Earth.

Eshu: Owner of the Crossroads. The Divine Messenger. Translator of the Language of Spirit to Humans and Language of Humans to Spirit. Opener of the Way.

Olokun: The Beginning of Consciousness. Power of the Unconscious Mind. Owner of the Ocean. Concept of Space.

Babaluaye: The Consciousnes of Cause and Effect. Father of the World. Moderation.

Yemaya: Consciousness of the Interconnectedness of All Things. Consciousness of Abundance. Owner of Salt Water Rivers. Owner of the Vegetative Part of the Ocean. Midwife.

Oshun: Consciousness of Love, Fertility, Abundance, and Knowledge. Spirit of the River. Law of Attraction

Shango: Consciousness of Passion. Owner of Lightning, Dance, and the Drum. Combination of the "White" of Obatala and the "Red" of Ogun. Courage. Male Virility.

Ogun: Consciousness of Iron. Consciousness of Analysis. Remover of Obstacles. Owner of Vitality. Force. The Guardian of Truth.

Oshosi: Consciousness of the Tracker. The Astral Traveler. The Hunter. Consciousness of the Archer, the Shortest Path to Spiritual Growth. Direction.

Obba: Consciousness of the Home. Consciousness of the Family and Domestic Life. Consciousness of Wisdom As Women Achieve Elderhood. Deep Female Mysticism.

Oya: Consciousness of Transformation. Consciousness of the Wind. Owner of the Energy of Storms, Thunder, Tornados, Hurricanes, the Marketplace, and Cemetaries. Change.

Ibeji: Consciousness of the Twins - The Twin Soul: one's human personality and spiritual personality, one residing on Earth, the other in the Spirit World. Abundance.

Osanyin: Consciousness of Plant Life. Owner of Herbal Medicine. Efficacy.

Egun: Our Ancestors. Whose Shoulders We Stand On.

Chapter 3

Glossary of Herbs Commonly Used in Ifá

Scientific Name/Nombre latino   ACHRAS ZAPOTA
Spanish Name/Nombre cubano   MAMEY COLORADO
Yoruba Name/Nombre lucumí   EMÍ

Scientific Name/Nombre latino   ACROCOMIA CRISPA (ELAEIS GUINEENSIS)
Spanish Name/Nombre cubano   COROJO
Yoruba Name/Nombre lucumí   EKPÓ, EPÓ, EPO PUPO, LUFI

Scientific Name/Nombre latino   ADENOROPIUM GOSSYPIFOLIUM
Spanish Name/Nombre cubano   FRAILECILLO, CAIRECILLO DE MONTE
Yoruba Name/Nombre lucumí   BASIGÜÉ, PÁIME

Scientific Name/Nombre latino   ADIANTUM TENERUM (ADIANTUM CAPILLUS VENERIS)
Spanish Name/Nombre cubano   CULANTRILLO DE POZO
Yoruba Name/Nombre lucumí   KOTONIO, OFI, NECENTÉN

Scientific Name/Nombre latino   ALLIUM CEPA
Spanish Name/Nombre cubano   CEBOLLA
Yoruba Name/Nombre lucumí   ALÚBOSA, ELLA SRO

Scientific Name/Nombre latino   ALLIUM SATIVUM
Spanish Name/Nombre cubano   AJO
Yoruba Name/Nombre lucumí   JOKOIO EWÉCO, ALU DESO GUERE

Scientific Name/Nombre latino   ALLOPHYLLUS COMINIA
Spanish Name/Nombre cubano   PALO CAJA
Yoruba Name/Nombre lucumí   IGGI BIRÉ, OÍN, MERÉMBE

Scientific Name/Nombre latino   ALPINIA AROMATICA (ALPINIA SPECIOSA SCHUM)
Spanish Name/Nombre cubano   COJATE, COATE, COLONIA
Yoruba Name/Nombre lucumí   ORÚ, OBURO, DIDONA

Scientific Name/Nombre latino   AMAIOUA CORYMBOSA
Spanish Name/Nombre cubano   PALO CAFÉ
Yoruba Name/Nombre lucumí   IGGIFERE, APÓ

Scientific Name/Nombre latino   AMARANTHUS VIRIDIS
Spanish Name/Nombre cubano   BLEDO
Yoruba Name/Nombre lucumí   LOBÉ, EWE TETÉ (CHAURÉ KUE KUE E WEIKO)

Scientific Name/Nombre latino   AMBROSIA ARTEMISIFOLIA (COCHLEARIA CORONOPUS)
Spanish Name/Nombre cubano   ALTAMISA, ARTEMISA
Yoruba Name/Nombre lucumí   LINIDDI

Scientific Name/Nombre latino   AMYRIS BALSAMIFERA
Spanish Name/Nombre cubano   CUABA
Yoruba Name/Nombre lucumí   LOASO

Scientific Name/Nombre latino   ANANAS ANANAS (ANANAS COMOSUS)
Spanish Name/Nombre cubano   PIÑA BLANCA
Yoruba Name/Nombre lucumí   EGBOIBO, OPPÓYIBO

Scientific Name/Nombre latino   ANNONA MURICATA
Spanish Name/Nombre cubano   GUANÁBANA
Yoruba Name/Nombre lucumí   IGGI OMÓ FUNFÚN, GWÁNILLO, NICHULARAFÚN

Scientific Name/Nombre latino   ANREDERA SPICATA (HEDERA HELIX)
Spanish Name/Nombre cubano   YEDRA
Yoruba Name/Nombre lucumí   ITAKO

Scientific Name/Nombre latino   ARACHIS HYPOGAEA
Spanish Name/Nombre cubano   MANÍ
Yoruba Name/Nombre lucumí   EPÁ, EPAMILBO, EFÁ, EWA, BUSIA

Scientific Name/Nombre latino   ARGEMONE MEXICANA
Spanish Name/Nombre cubano   CARDO SANTO
Yoruba Name/Nombre lucumí   IKÁ, AGOGÓ, IGBEELEGÚN, EEKANNA EKUN

Scientific Name/Nombre latino   ARTEMISIA ABROTANUM (ARTEMISIA CAMPHORATA)
Spanish Name/Nombre cubano   INCIENSO
Yoruba Name/Nombre lucumí   TURARÉ, MINSELO

Scientific Name/Nombre latino   IPOMOEA BATATAS
Spanish Name/Nombre cubano   BONIATO
Yoruba Name/Nombre lucumí   UNDUKÚMDUKÚ, KUÁNDUKU, ODUKÓ, CUCÚNDU
                                   CUENDÚEN, CUCUNDUCÚ, CUCUDUCÚ

Scientific Name/Nombre latino   BIXA ORELLANA
Spanish Name/Nombre cubano   BIJA
Yoruba Name/Nombre lucumí   OEN

Scientific Name/Nombre latino   CALALU
Spanish Name/Nombre cubano   CALALÚ
Yoruba Name/Nombre lucumí   CALALÚ

Scientific Name/Nombre latino   CALYCOPHILLUM CANDIDISSIMUM
Spanish Name/Nombre cubano   DÁGAME
Yoruba Name/Nombre lucumí   LIONSE

Scientific Name/Nombre latino   CAMERARIA LATIFOLIA
Spanish Name/Nombre cubano   MABOA
Yoruba Name/Nombre lucumí   LÉCHU IBAYÉ

Scientific Name/Nombre latino   CAPRARIA BIFLORA
Spanish Name/Nombre cubano   ESCLABIOSA, ESCLAVIOSA
Yoruba Name/Nombre lucumí   GAÚTI

Scientific Name/Nombre latino   CAPSICUM BAC CATUM
Spanish Name/Nombre cubano   AJÍ GUAGUAO
Yoruba Name/Nombre lucumí   ATÁ, GUAGUAO

Scientific Name/Nombre latino   CARICA PAPAYA
Spanish Name/Nombre cubano   FRUTA BOMBA, PAPAYA
Yoruba Name/Nombre lucumí   IDEFÉ, IBEKUÉ, IBÉPPE

Scientific Name/Nombre latino   CASEARIA HIRSUTA
Spanish Name/Nombre cubano   RASPA LENGUA
Yoruba Name/Nombre lucumí   EWE ELÉNU, YERÉOBO

Scientific Name/Nombre latino   CASSIA OCCIDENTALIS (CASSIA TORA)
Spanish Name/Nombre cubano   GUANINA, HIERBA HEDIONDA
Yoruba Name/Nombre lucumí   JASISAN KROPOMU, YAASO, JARA–JARA, AYEGUÉ,
                                   OYÉUN, OYEUSÁ, JARA-JARA, EWE TOMODE

Scientific Name/Nombre latino   CECROPIA PELTATA
Spanish Name/Nombre cubano   YAGRUMA
Yoruba Name/Nombre lucumí   IGGI, OGGUGÚ, OGUGUN, OGÚN GUN, OGGÚ, LORO,
                                   LARA, LARO

Scientific Name/Nombre latino   CEDRELA MEXICANA (CITRUS MEDICA)
Spanish Name/Nombre cubano   CEDRO
Yoruba Name/Nombre lucumí   OPEPÉ, ROKÓ

Scientific Name/Nombre latino   CEIBA PENTANDRA (CEIBA CASEARIA)
Spanish Name/Nombre cubano   CEIBA
Yoruba Name/Nombre lucumí   ARABBÁ, ALABA, ARÁGGUO, IROKO, IROKO TERÉ,
                                   IROKO–AWO, ELÚWERE, ELUÉCO, ASABÁ (IGGI ARABBÁ),
                                   IGGI OLORUN

Scientific Name/Nombre latino   CELOSIA ARGENTEA
Spanish Name/Nombre cubano   CRESTA DE GALLO
Yoruba Name/Nombre lucumí   LIBBE KUKO

Scientific Name/Nombre latino   CESTRUM DIURNUM
Spanish Name/Nombre cubano   GALÁN DE DÍA
Yoruba Name/Nombre lucumí   ORUFIRÍN, TOÍRO

Scientific Name/Nombre latino   CINNAMOMUM CASSIA (CINNAMOMUM ZEYLANICUM)
Spanish Name/Nombre cubano   CANELA DE MONTE, CANELA DE CHINA
Yoruba Name/Nombre lucumí   IGGI EPÓ KAN, DEDÉ, KOROKOLO

Scientific Name/Nombre latino   CISSUS SICYOIDES (CISSUS QUADRANDOLARIS)
Spanish Name/Nombre cubano   BEJUCO UBÍ, BEJUCO UVÍ
Yoruba Name/Nombre lucumí   EGGUÉLE KERI

Scientific Name/Nombre latino   CITRULLUS CITRULLUS (CITRULLUS LANATUS)
Spanish Name/Nombre cubano   MELÓN DE AGUA
Yoruba Name/Nombre lucumí   AGBÉYE, AGUE TUTÚ, ITAKÚN, OYÉ, OGGURE, EGURIN

Scientific Name/Nombre latino   CITRUS AURANTIUM (CITRUS SINENSIS)
Spanish Name/Nombre cubano   NARANJA
Yoruba Name/Nombre lucumí   OROLOCUM, ORÓMBO, OLÓMBO, OSÁN, ORMBO,
                                   OBBURUKÚ, OSAEYÍMBO, ESÁ

Scientific Name/Nombre latino   CITRUS AURANTIUM, VAR. AMARA (CITRUS VULGARIS)
Spanish Name/Nombre cubano   NARANJA AGRIA
Yoruba Name/Nombre lucumí   KOROSÁN

Scientific Name/Nombre latino   CITRUS LIMON
Spanish Name/Nombre cubano   LIMÓN
Yoruba Name/Nombre lucumí   ORÓCO, OROMBOUEUÉ, OLÓMBO

Scientific Name/Nombre latino	CHENOPODIUM AMBROSIODES
Spanish Name/Nombre cubano	APASOTE
Yoruba Name/Nombre lucumí	OLINE

Scientific Name/Nombre latino	CHRYSOPHILLUM CAINITO
Spanish Name/Nombre cubano	CAIMITO
Yoruba Name/Nombre lucumí	ASÁN, ALLÉCOFOLE, OSÁM, OGÓE FUSÉ, AYÉCO FOLÉ

Scientific Name/Nombre latino	COCOS NUCIFERA
Spanish Name/Nombre cubano	COCO
Yoruba Name/Nombre lucumí	OBI

Scientific Name/Nombre latino	COFFEA ARABICA
Spanish Name/Nombre cubano	CAFÉ
Yoruba Name/Nombre lucumí	OBIMOTIGWÁ, IGGI KAN, EKÁNCHACHAETÉ, OMATIWAOSEGÜi, OSINA BONA, OMÍ DUDU

Scientific Name/Nombre latino	COMMELINA ELEGANS
Spanish Name/Nombre cubano	CANUTILLO
Yoruba Name/Nombre lucumí	KARODO, KORODO, CARRODDO, CARODI COTONÉMBO, COTONEMBO, COTOLO, IBAKUÁ MINOCUÍ, MINI

Scientific Name/Nombre latino	CORCHORUS OLITORIUS
Spanish Name/Nombre cubano	MALVA TÈ, GUENGUERÉ
Yoruba Name/Nombre lucumí	EFO

Scientific Name/Nombre latino	CORCHORUS SILIQUOSUS
Yoruba Name/Nombre lucumí	DEDÉ

Scientific Name/Nombre latino	CORDIA COLLOCOCCA
Spanish Name/Nombre cubano	ATEJE COMUN
Yoruba Name/Nombre lucumí	LACHEO, LÁNGWE

Scientific Name/Nombre latino	CRESCENTIA CUJETE
Spanish Name/Nombre cubano	GÜIRA
Yoruba Name/Nombre lucumí	EGGWÁ, IGBÁ, AGBÉ, AGGÜÉ, EGWÁ

Scientific Name/Nombre latino	CUCURBITA MAXIMA
Spanish Name/Nombre cubano	CALABAZA
Yoruba Name/Nombre lucumí	ELEGUEDDÉ

Scientific Name/Nombre latino	CUPANIA CUBENSIS
Spanish Name/Nombre cubano	GUARA
Yoruba Name/Nombre lucumí	GUARÁ, AGAGWÁN

Scientific Name/Nombre latino	CURCAS CURCAS (JATROPHA CURCAS)
Spanish Name/Nombre cubano	PIÑON BOTIJA
Yoruba Name/Nombre lucumí	ADDÓ, ALUMOFÓ, AKUNU, OLOBOTUYA, OLÉ IYÉTEBE

Scientific Name/Nombre latino	CYNODON DACTYLON (AGROPYRUM REPENS)
Spanish Name/Nombre cubano	GRAMA, PATA DE GALLINA
Yoruba Name/Nombre lucumí	COTONEMBO, ERAN, DENGO, ELEGGUÉ, TUMAYÁ, IYERÁN

Scientific Name/Nombre latino DATURA STRAMONIUM
Spanish Name/Nombre cubano CHAMICO, TÉ DEL DIABLO
Yoruba Name/Nombre lucumí EWE OFÓ, EWE ECHÉNLA

Scientific Name/Nombre latino DATURA SUAVEOLENS
Spanish Name/Nombre cubano CAMPANA
Yoruba Name/Nombre lucumí AGGOGÓ, AGOGÓ

Scientific Name/Nombre latino DIOSCOREA ALATA
Spanish Name/Nombre cubano ÑAME BLANCO
Yoruba Name/Nombre lucumí ICHÚ, OSÚRA

Scientific Name/Nombre latino DIOSCOREA PILOSIUSCULA
Spanish Name/Nombre cubano ÑAME VOLADOR, ÑAME CIMARRÓN
Yoruba Name/Nombre lucumí ICHÚ

Scientific Name/Nombre latino EICHHORNIA AZUREA (EICHHORNIA CRASSIPES,
  PONTEDERIA CRASSIPES)
Spanish Name/Nombre cubano FLOR DE AGUA
Yoruba Name/Nombre lucumí OLLUORO, OLLÓURO, TANÁ FÚN FÚN, BODÓ

Scientific Name/Nombre latino ELAPHRIUM SIMARUBA (BURSERA SIMARUBA)
Spanish Name/Nombre cubano ALMÁCIGO
Yoruba Name/Nombre lucumí IGGI ADDAMA, MOYÉ, ILÚKI

Scientific Name/Nombre latino ELEUSINE INDICA (DACTYLOCTENIUM AEGYPTIUM)
Spanish Name/Nombre cubano PATA DE GALLINA
Yoruba Name/Nombre lucumí ERÁN, DEDÉ, ARÁOGU, OKLEPÚESU

Scientific Name/Nombre latino ERYTHRINA GLAUCA (ERYTHRINA BERTEROANA)
Spanish Name/Nombre cubano PIÑON DE PITO
Yoruba Name/Nombre lucumí EFÉKE, YRIN

Scientific Name/Nombre latino EUPATORIUM ODORATUM (EUPATORIUM CANNABINUM)
Spanish Name/Nombre cubano ALBAHACA DE SABANA, TRAVESERA, ALBAHAQUILLA,
  ROMPE ZARAGÜEY
Yoruba Name/Nombre lucumí TABATÉ, JAN

Scientific Name/Nombre latino EUPHORBIA LACTEA (EUPHORBIA PEPLUS)
Spanish Name/Nombre cubano CARDÓN
Yoruba Name/Nombre lucumí IKÁ, AGOGÓ

Scientific Name/Nombre latino EUPHORBIA PULCHERRIMA
Spanish Name/Nombre cubano FLOR DE PASCUA

Scientific Name/Nombre latino FICUS MEMBRANACEA
Spanish Name/Nombre cubano JAGÜEY
Yoruba Name/Nombre lucumí FIAPABBA, IGGI IGWÁ, IGGI OKÉ, AFOMÁ, UENDO

Scientific Name/Nombre latino FICUS NITIDA
Spanish Name/Nombre cubano LAUREL DE INDIA
Yoruba Name/Nombre lucumí IGGINILE ITIRI, IGGI GAFIOFO

Scientific Name/Nombre latino FICUS RELIGIOSA
Spanish Name/Nombre cubano ÁLAMO
Yoruba Name/Nombre lucumí OFÁ, IGOLE, ABAILA, LLESO, IGGOLÉ, IKIYÉNYO, OFÁ

Scientific Name/Nombre latino GOSSYPIUM BARBADENSE
Spanish Name/Nombre cubano ALGODÓN
Yoruba Name/Nombre lucumí ORI ORO, EU, OÚ, OWÚ, KEOLI

Scientific Name/Nombre latino GOUANIA POLYGAMA
Spanish Name/Nombre cubano BEJUCO LEÑATERO, BEJUCO DE CUBA
Yoruba Name/Nombre lucumí IDALLA

Scientific Name/Nombre latino GUAJUMA ULMIFOLIA (GUAZUMA GUAZUMA)
Spanish Name/Nombre cubano GUÁSIMA
Yoruba Name/Nombre lucumí IGGI BONI

Scientific Name/Nombre latino HELIOTROPIUM INDICUM (ELIOTROPIUM CAMPECHIANUM)
Spanish Name/Nombre cubano ALACRANCILLO
Yoruba Name/Nombre lucumí AGUÉYI

Scientific Name/Nombre latino HIBISCUS ABELMOSCHUS (ABELMOSCHUS ESCULENTUS)
Spanish Name/Nombre cubano AMBARINA
Yoruba Name/Nombre lucumí IYEYÉ-TANAEKO

Scientific Name/Nombre latino HIBISCUS ESCULENTUS
Spanish Name/Nombre cubano QUIMBOMBÓ
Yoruba Name/Nombre lucumí LILÁ, ALILÁ, ILÁ, ALLÁ

Scientific Name/Nombre latino HIBISCUS ROSA-SINENSIS
Spanish Name/Nombre cubano HIBISCU o MAR PACIFICO
Yoruba Name/Nombre lucumí EWE ATÒRI

Scientific Name/Nombre latino ILEX AQUIFOLIUM (ILEX MONTANA)
Spanish Name/Nombre cubano ACEBO DE SIERRA, ACEBO DE TIERRA
Yoruba Name/Nombre lucumí SUCUÍ

Scientific Name/Nombre latino INDIGOFERA TINCTORIA
Spanish Name/Nombre cubano AÑIL, INDIGO
Yoruba Name/Nombre lucumí YINIYA, ÑI

Scientific Name/Nombre latino IPOMOEA TUBEROSA
Spanish Name/Nombre cubano BEJUCO DE INDIO
Yoruba Name/Nombre lucumí CHINYO

Scientific Name/Nombre latino JAMBOS JAMBOS (EUGENIA JAMBOS, EUGENIA
CARYIOPHILLATA, JAMBOSA CARYOPHYLLUS,
CARYOPHYLLUS AROMATICUS)
Spanish Name/Nombre cubano POMARROSA
Yoruba Name/Nombre lucumí YILEBO, ECHICACHO

Scientific Name/Nombre latino JATROPHA DIVERSIFOLIA
Spanish Name/Nombre cubano PEREGRINA
Yoruba Name/Nombre lucumí ERO

Scientific Name/Nombre latino LACTUCA SATIVA (LACTUCA SCARIOLA)
Spanish Name/Nombre cubano LECHUGA
Yoruba Name/Nombre lucumí ILENKE, OGGÚ YÉYÉ

Scientific Name/Nombre latino	LAGERSTROEMIA INDICA
Spanish Name/Nombre cubano	ASTRONOMIA
Yoruba Name/Nombre lucumí	TAKÉ

Scientific Name/Nombre latino	LEPIDIUM VIRGINICUM
Spanish Name/Nombre cubano	MASTUERZO, SABE LECCIÓN
Yoruba Name/Nombre lucumí	ERIBO, ICHINI-CHINI, ERIBOSA, TÁN

Scientific Name/Nombre latino	LEUCAENA GLAUCA
Spanish Name/Nombre cubano	AROMA BLANCA
Yoruba Name/Nombre lucumí	RIANI

Scientific Name/Nombre latino	LONCHOCARPUS LATIFOLIUS
Spanish Name/Nombre cubano	GUAMÁ DE COSTA
Yoruba Name/Nombre lucumí	YERÉKETE, ADERE ODO

Scientific Name/Nombre latino	LYCOPERSICUM ESCULENTUM
Spanish Name/Nombre cubano	TOMATE
Yoruba Name/Nombre lucumí	ICHOMA, ICAN, ICARE, YKAIE

Scientific Name/Nombre latino	MANGIFERA INDICA
Spanish Name/Nombre cubano	MANGO
Yoruba Name/Nombre lucumí	AIRO, ORO, ELÉSO, ORUN BÉKE, ORO AYIMBO, OLOMBO

Scientific Name/Nombre latino	MANIHOT ESCULENTA
Spanish Name/Nombre cubano	YUCA
Yoruba Name/Nombre lucumí	KOKOMADOCO, IBAGGUDDÁN, BAGGUDÁN

Scientific Name/Nombre latino	MELIA AZEDERACH
Spanish Name/Nombre cubano	PARAÍSO
Yoruba Name/Nombre lucumí	IBAYO, YIYA

Scientific Name/Nombre latino	MELOTHRIA GUADALUPENSIS
Spanish Name/Nombre cubano	MELONCILLO

Scientific Name/Nombre latino	MIMOSA PUDICA
Spanish Name/Nombre cubano	SENSITIVA, VERGONZOSA, DORMIDERA
Yoruba Name/Nombre lucumí	ERAN KUMI, ERAN LOYÓ, OMIMI, YARANIMÓ

Scientific Name/Nombre latino	MUSA PARADISIACA
Spanish Name/Nombre cubano	PLATANO
Yoruba Name/Nombre lucumí	OGGUEDÉ, OGUE GUERE

Scientific Name/Nombre latino	NASTURTIUM OFFICINALE
Spanish Name/Nombre cubano	BERRO
Yoruba Name/Nombre lucumí	IGUÉRE, YEYÉ PEREGÚN

Scientific Name/Nombre latino	NICOTIANA TABACUM, Var. HAVANENSIS
Spanish Name/Nombre cubano	TABACO
Yoruba Name/Nombre lucumí	ETÁBA, ACHÁ

Scientific Name/Nombre latino	OCIMUM BASILICUM, Var. ANISATUM
Spanish Name/Nombre cubano	ALBAHACA ANISADA
Yoruba Name/Nombre lucumí	TONÓMIYO, ORORÓ, NISÉ

Scientific Name/Nombre latino   OCIMUM BASILICUM, VAR. PURPUREUM
Spanish Name/Nombre cubano   ALBAHACA MORADA
Yoruba Name/Nombre lucumí   ORORÓ, FINI ADACHÉ

Scientific Name/Nombre latino   OCIMUM MICRANTHUM
Spanish Name/Nombre cubano   ALBAHACA DE CLAVO
Yoruba Name/Nombre lucumí   BERENRÉ, ORORÓ

Scientific Name/Nombre latino   OCIMUM SANCTUM (CLINOPODIUM VULGARE)
Spanish Name/Nombre cubano   ALBAHACA CIMARRONA
Yoruba Name/Nombre lucumí   ORORÓ

Scientific Name/Nombre latino   OREODOXA REGIA (ROYSTONEA REGIA)
Spanish Name/Nombre cubano   PALMA REAL
Yoruba Name/Nombre lucumí   ILÉ CHANGÓ ORISSÁ, IGGI OPPWÉ, OPÉ, ALABI, CEFIDIYÉ, ELUWERE, OLUWEKÓN

Scientific Name/Nombre latino   ORIZA SATIVA
Spanish Name/Nombre cubano   ARROZ
Yoruba Name/Nombre lucumí   EUO, SINCOFA, IRÁSI, CHEQUEFA

Scientific Name/Nombre latino   OXANDRA LANCEOLATA
Spanish Name/Nombre cubano   YAYA
Yoruba Name/Nombre lucumí   YAYA, ECHI

Scientific Name/Nombre latino   PARALABATIA DICTYONEURA
Spanish Name/Nombre cubano   CUCUYO
Yoruba Name/Nombre lucumí   OFUNTANA

Scientific Name/Nombre latino   PARITI TILIACEUM
Spanish Name/Nombre cubano   MAJAGUA
Yoruba Name/Nombre lucumí   MERENGUENE

Scientific Name/Nombre latino   PARTHENIUM HYSTEROPHORUS
Spanish Name/Nombre cubano   ARTEMISILLA
Yoruba Name/Nombre lucumí   EWE IRII

Scientific Name/Nombre latino   PELARGONIUM ODARATISSIMUM
Spanish Name/Nombre cubano   GERANIO
Yoruba Name/Nombre lucumí   PUPAYO

Scientific Name/Nombre latino   PERSEA GRATISSIMA
Spanish Name/Nombre cubano   AGUACATE
Yoruba Name/Nombre lucumí   ITOBI, OKUTARA ITÓBI, ODOFRE, BIMA, ACATARA

Scientific Name/Nombre latino   PETIVERIA ALLIACEA
Spanish Name/Nombre cubano   ANAMÚ
Yoruba Name/Nombre lucumí   YENA, ANAMÚ, OCHISÁN

Scientific Name/Nombre latino   PETROSELINUM CRISPUM
Spanish Name/Nombre cubano   PEREJIL
Yoruba Name/Nombre lucumí   ISAKO, IYADEDÉ

Scientific Name/Nombre latino   PHYLLANTUS ACIDUS (CICCA DISTICHA)
Yoruba Name/Nombre lucumí   MEYELÉ, ESO, AKIVARÉ

Scientific Name/Nombre latino   PHYLLANTUS NIRURI
Spanish Name/Nombre cubano   HIERBA DE LA NIÑA
Yoruba Name/Nombre lucumí   NENE, NANI, ÑANI, ÑENÉ

Scientific Name/Nombre latino   AFRAMOMUN MELEGUETA
Spanish Name/Nombre cubano   PIMIENTA DE GUINEA
Yoruba Name/Nombre lucumí   ATÁ, ATARE

Scientific Name/Nombre latino   PINUS TROPICALIS (PINUS CORIBEA)
Spanish Name/Nombre cubano   PINO
Yoruba Name/Nombre lucumí   OKILÓN, ORUKOÑIKÁN, YEMAO

Scientific Name/Nombre latino   PIPER ADUNCUM
Spanish Name/Nombre cubano   PLATANILLO DE CUBA
Yoruba Name/Nombre lucumí   OLÚBBO

Scientific Name/Nombre latino   PISONIA ACULEATA
Spanish Name/Nombre cubano   ZARZA
Yoruba Name/Nombre lucumí   EGUN, IGGI EGÚN, TIYÁ

Scientific Name/Nombre latino   PITHECOLOBIUM ARBOREUM
Spanish Name/Nombre cubano   MORURO
Yoruba Name/Nombre lucumí   ORUDAN, EFENKOKO

Scientific Name/Nombre latino   PLANTAGO
Spanish Name/Nombre cubano   LLANTEN O YANTEN

Scientific Name/Nombre latino   PLUMBAGO SCADENS (CORDIA GLOBOSA)
Spanish Name/Nombre cubano   LEGAÑA, LAGAÑA DE AURA
Yoruba Name/Nombre lucumí   IWAGO, ICOLEKOKÉ

Scientific Name/Nombre latino   POEPPIGIA PROCERA
Spanish Name/Nombre cubano   TÉNGUE, PALO TENGUE
Yoruba Name/Nombre lucumí   ADEBESÚ, SONGA, LABAL, LABARÍ

Scientific Name/Nombre latino   POINCIANA PULCHERRIMA
Spanish Name/Nombre cubano   GUACAMAYA AMARILLA
Yoruba Name/Nombre lucumí   ORUMAYA, PUPURUSA

Scientific Name/Nombre latino   POINCIANA PULCHERRIMA
Spanish Name/Nombre cubano   GUACAMAYA COLORADA
Yoruba Name/Nombre lucumí   ORUMAYA, EWE PON, KAMARERÉ, ERUNTOKO

Scientific Name/Nombre latino   PORTULACA OLERACEA
Spanish Name/Nombre cubano   VERDOLAGA
Yoruba Name/Nombre lucumí   EKISÁN, PAPASAN

Scientific Name/Nombre latino   PROSOPIS CHILENSIS
Spanish Name/Nombre cubano   ALGARROBO
Yoruba Name/Nombre lucumí   EWE BÁNA

Scientific Name/Nombre latino   PRUNUS OCCIDENTALIS
Spanish Name/Nombre cubano   CUAJANI
Yoruba Name/Nombre lucumí   MADDETÉO

Scientific Name/Nombre latino   PSIDIUM GUAYAVA
Spanish Name/Nombre cubano   GUAYABA
Yoruba Name/Nombre lucumí   KENKU

Scientific Name/Nombre latino   PUNICA GRANATUM
Spanish Name/Nombre cubano   GRANADA
Yoruba Name/Nombre lucumí   OROCO, MAYAKU, YAYEKU, KANSORE, CHIMINÍ
                                                     CHIMINÍ, AGBÁ

Scientific Name/Nombre latino   RHIZOPHORA MANGLE (AVICENNA NITIDA,
                                                     RHIZOPHORA CANDEL)
Spanish Name/Nombre cubano   MANGLE
Yoruba Name/Nombre lucumí   EWE ATÍODO, KASIORO

Scientific Name/Nombre latino   RHOEO DISCOLOR (RHOEO SPATHACEA, TRADESCANTIA
                                                     DISCOLOR)
Spanish Name/Nombre cubano   CORDOBÁN, CORDOVÁN
Yoruba Name/Nombre lucumí   PEREGÚN TUPÁ, PEREGÚN PUPPUÁ, PERUGÚN, TUPÁ,
                                                     DIELA, YERE GUN

Scientific Name/Nombre latino   ROSA GALLICA
Spanish Name/Nombre cubano   ROSA FRANCESA
Yoruba Name/Nombre lucumí   TETELÍ, DIDEKERÉ

Scientific Name/Nombre latino   ROSMARINUS OFFICINALIS
Spanish Name/Nombre cubano   ROMERO
Yoruba Name/Nombre lucumí   RE, PAGWABIMÁ

Scientific Name/Nombre latino   ROUREA GLABRA
Spanish Name/Nombre cubano   MATANEGRO
Yoruba Name/Nombre lucumí   KONRI, KUKENKÉLEYO

Scientific Name/Nombre latino   RUTA CHALEPENSIS
Spanish Name/Nombre cubano   RUDA
Yoruba Name/Nombre lucumí   ATOPÁ KUN

Scientific Name/Nombre latino   SACCHARUM OFFICINARUM
Spanish Name/Nombre cubano   CAÑA DE AZÚCAR
Yoruba Name/Nombre lucumí   IGGUERÉ, IREKE, OREKÉ, EREKÉ

Scientific Name/Nombre latino   SAGITTARIA INTERMEDIA
Spanish Name/Nombre cubano   MALANGUILLA, SÁCU-SÁCU
Yoruba Name/Nombre lucumí   KÓHO

Scientific Name/Nombre latino   SALVIA OFFICINALIS (SALVIA SCLAREA)
Spanish Name/Nombre cubano   SALVIA DE CASTILLA
Yoruba Name/Nombre lucumí   KIRIWI

Scientific Name/Nombre latino   SAPONARIA OFFICINALIS (GOUANIA LUPULOIDES,
                                                     GOUANIA POLYGAMA)
Spanish Name/Nombre cubano   JABONCILLO
Yoruba Name/Nombre lucumí   OBUENO, KEKERIONGO

Scientific Name/Nombre latino   SAVIA SESSILLIFLORA
Spanish Name/Nombre cubano   ARETILLO
Yoruba Name/Nombre lucumí   GUANKÉ

Scientific Name/Nombre latino   SCHAEFFERIA FRUTESCENS
Spanish Name/Nombre cubano   AMANSA GUAPO
Yoruba Name/Nombre lucumí   KUNINO

Scientific Name/Nombre latino   SERJANIA LUPULINA (SERJANIA DIVERSIFOLIA)
Spanish Name/Nombre cubano   BEJUCO COLORADO
Yoruba Name/Nombre lucumí   OBOLÓ

Scientific Name/Nombre latino   SERJANIA PANICULATA
Spanish Name/Nombre cubano   BEJUCO DE CORRALES
Yoruba Name/Nombre lucumí   WÁNIRI

Scientific Name/Nombre latino   SESAMUM INDICUM
Spanish Name/Nombre cubano   AJONJOLÍ
Yoruba Name/Nombre lucumí   AMATI

Scientific Name/Nombre latino   SIMARUBA GLAUCA
Spanish Name/Nombre cubano   PALO BLANCO
Yoruba Name/Nombre lucumí   IGGI FÚN

Scientific Name/Nombre latino   SOLANUM HAVANENSE
Spanish Name/Nombre cubano   AJÍ DE CHINA
Yoruba Name/Nombre lucumí   ATÁ GUARÚ, ATÁ FINLANDI

Scientific Name/Nombre latino   SOLANUM NIGRUM (SOLANUM AMERICANUM, SOLANUM
    MODIFLURUM)
Spanish Name/Nombre cubano   HIERBA MORA
Yoruba Name/Nombre lucumí   ATORE, ATORÍ, EFODA, EPODÚ, EGUNMO

Scientific Name/Nombre latino   SPIGELIA ANTHELMIA
Spanish Name/Nombre cubano   ESPIGELIS
Yoruba Name/Nombre lucumí   MINIRÉ

Scientific Name/Nombre latino   SWIETENI MOHAGONY
Spanish Name/Nombre cubano   CAOBA
Yoruba Name/Nombre lucumí   AYÁN, ROCO

Scientific Name/Nombre latino   TERMINALIA CATAPPA (TERMINALIA GLAUCESCENS,
    TERMINALIA IVORENSIS)
Spanish Name/Nombre cubano   ALMENDRO
Yoruba Name/Nombre lucumí   ABUSÍ, IGGI, URÉ, ECUCI

Scientific Name/Nombre latino   TERMINALIA INTERMEDIA
Spanish Name/Nombre cubano   CHICHARRÓN DE MONTE
Yoruba Name/Nombre lucumí   YENKÉ

Scientific Name/Nombre latino   TOURNEFORTIA GNAPHALODES
Spanish Name/Nombre cubano   INCIENSO DE PLAYA
Yoruba Name/Nombre lucumí   EGBADDÓ

Scientific Name/Nombre latino   TRIBULUS MAXIMUS
Spanish Name/Nombre cubano   ABROJO
Yoruba Name/Nombre lucumí   EGBELEGÚN, IGGILEGÚN

Scientific Name/Nombre latino   TRIBULUS MAXIMUS (KALSTROEMIA MAXIMA)
Spanish Name/Nombre cubano   ABROJO TERRESTRE
Yoruba Name/Nombre lucumí   CHORO, IGBELEGGÚN

Scientific Name/Nombre latino   TRICHILIA HAVANENSIS
Spanish Name/Nombre cubano   SIGUARAYA, CIGUARAYA
Yoruba Name/Nombre lucumí   ATORI

Scientific Name/Nombre latino   TRICHILIA HIRTA
Spanish Name/Nombre cubano   CABO DE HACHA
Yoruba Name/Nombre lucumí   ERÉ, IGGI NIKÁ, AKUDÍYICA

Scientific Name/Nombre latino   VIGNA UNGUICULATA (DOLICHOS SINENSIS, DOLICHOS
                                   LABLAB)
Spanish Name/Nombre cubano   FRIJOL DE CARITA
Yoruba Name/Nombre lucumí   ERE-É PIPÁ, ERECHÉ

Scientific Name/Nombre latino   VITEX DONIANA
Spanish Name/Nombre cubano   OFÓN, OFÚN
Yoruba Name/Nombre lucumí   MEREMIYÉ

Scientific Name/Nombre latino   VITIS TILLIFOLIA
Spanish Name/Nombre cubano   BEJUCO JÍMAGUA, PARRA CIMARRONA
Yoruba Name/Nombre lucumí   LOPAMÓ, AJARÁ MELLI

Scientific Name/Nombre latino   XANTHOSOMA SAGITTIFOLIUM (XANTHOSOMA
                                   VIOLACEUM, COLOCASIA ATIQUORUM)
Spanish Name/Nombre cubano   MALANGA
Yoruba Name/Nombre lucumí   IKOKU, ICHU, CHICÁ, COCO, LLESCO, MARABABO

Scientific Name/Nombre latino   ZANTHOXYLUM MARTINICENSE
Spanish Name/Nombre cubano   AYÚA
Yoruba Name/Nombre lucumí   ELEGÚN, IGGI ORO

Scientific Name/Nombre latino   ZEA MAIS
Spanish Name/Nombre cubano   MAIZ
Yoruba Name/Nombre lucumí   AGUADÓ, AGUADDÓ, AGGUADÓ, ABÁDDO, AWADO,
                                   OKÁ

Scientific Name/Nombre latino   ZEBRINA PURPUSII (ZEBRINA PENDULA, TRADESCANZIA
                                   TRICOLOR)
Spanish Name/Nombre cubano   CUCARACHA (ZEBRINA PENDULA), CUCARACHA
                                   MORADA (ZEBRINA PURPUSII)
Yoruba Name/Nombre lucumí   AÑAÍ

Scientific Name/Nombre Latino   PILEA MICROPHYLLA, L.
Spanish Name/Nombre cubano   FRESCURA
Yoruba Name/Nombre lucumí   KUYEKUYE, EDUN, EWE TUTU

Scientific Name/Nombre latino   CATHARANTHUS ROSEUS
Spanish Name/Nombre cubano   VICARIA

Scientific Name/Nombre latino   SIDA CORDATA
Spanish Name/Nombre cubano   BOTÓN DE ORO
Yoruba Name/Nombre lucumi   EWE FIN, EWE OFIN

Scientific Name/Nombre latino   PASPALUM NOTATUM
Spanish Name/Nombre cubano   HIERBA FINA
Yoruba Name/Nombre lucumi   EWÉ GBEGÍ

Scientific Name/Nombre latino   EUPATORIUM VILLOSUM
Spanish Name/Nombre cubano   ABRE CAMINO

Scientific Name/Nombre latino   MORINGA OLEIFERA
Spanish Name/Nombre cubano   ACACIA, PARAISO BLANCO

Scientific Name/Nombre latino   BOERHAAVIA ERECTA CARIBAEA
Spanish Name/Nombre cubano   ATIPONLA
Nombre lucumi   ATIPONLA

Scientific Name/Nombre latino   PIPER PELTATUM L.
Spanish Name/Nombre cubano   CAISIMÓN
Yoruba Name/Nombre lucumi   EWÉ BENERÍ, EWÉ ÒTÓ

Scientific Name/Nombre latino   BAMBUSA VULGARIS
Nombre cubano   CAÑA BRAVA

Scientific Name/Nombre latino   MOMORDICA CHARANTIA L
Spanish Name/Nombre cubano   CUNDE AMOR, AMOR SECO, ROMERILLO
Yoruba Name/Nombre lucumi   ABERE OLOKO, ABARE, OJU AGUTAN

Scientific Name/Nombre latino   RICINUS COMMUNIS
Spanish Name/Nombre cubano   TARTAGO, HIGUERETA
Yoruba Name/Nombre lucumí   EWÉ ÒMÒ

Scientific Name/Nombre latino   LAVANDULA ANGUSTIFOLIA
Spanish Name/Nombre cubano   LAVANDA

Scientific Name/Nombre latino   PENNYWORT
Spanish Name/Nombre cubano   PARAGUITA
Yoruba Name/Nombre lucumi   EWÉ AKÒKO

Scientific Name/Nombre latino   MIRABILIS JALAPA
Spanish Name/Nombre cubano   MARAVILLA
Yoruba Name/Nombre lucumi   EWÉ ÒGUMO, EWÉ TANAPOSHO

Scientific Name/Nombre latino   ACHRAS SAPOTE
Spanish Name/Nombre cubano   ZAPOTE

Scientific Name/Nombre latino   VERBENA OFFICINALIS
Spanish Name/Nombre cubano   VERBENA
Yoruba Name/Nombre lucumi   EWÉ OGÁNGÁN

Scientific Name/Nombre latino   CISSAMPELOS OWARIENSISE O CISSAMPELOS
                                     MUCRONATA
Spanish Name/Nombre cubano   DEJAME SENTARME

Scientific Name/Nombre latino   KALANCHOE PINNATA
Spanish Name/Nombre cubano   SIEMPRE VIVA, PRODIGIOSA O BELLADONA
Yoruba Name/Nombre lucumi   EWÉ DUNDUN, EWÉ ODUNDUN

Scientific Name/Nombre latino   ABRUS PRECATORIUS
Spanish Name/Nombre cubano   PEONÍA
Yoruba Name/Nombre lucumi   EWERENJENJÉ

Scientific Name/Nombre latino   NYMPHAEA LOTUS
Spanish Name/Nombre cubano   LIRIO DE AGUA O FLOR DE LOTO
Yoruba Name/Nombre lucumi   ASHIBATA

Scientific Name/Nombre latino   PISTIA STRATIOTES
Spanish Name/Nombre cubano   LECHUGUILLA
Yoruba Name/Nombre lucumi   OJU ORO

Scientific Name/Nombre latino   CAESALPINIA BONDUC
Spanish Name/Nombre cubano   QUITA MALDICIÓN
Yoruba Name/Nombre lucumi   EWE AYO, ABERIKUNLÓ

Scientific Name/Nombre latino   AMARANTHUS CAUDATUS
Yoruba Name/Nombre lucumi   EWE TELE

Chapter 4

List of Trees Commonly Used to Make Palos

1. Vencedor

2. Palo hueso

3. Algarrobo

4. Pimiento de costa

5. Yagruma

6. Jaguey

7. Amansa guapo

8. Raspa lengua

9. Moruro

10. Sauco

11. Alejo

12. Abre camino

13. Varia

14. Parami

15. Malabo

16. Yamao

17. Pino

18. Rompe camisa

19. Guacamaya

20. Yo puedo mas quetu

21. Guayabo